The Word on Management

A Topical Index of Scriptures for Managers and Employees

Second Edition

by
Dr. John Mulford
and
Bruce Winston

WIPF & STOCK · Eugene, Oregon

Resource Publications
A division of Wipf and Stock Publishers
199 W 8th Ave, Suite 3
Eugene, OR 97401

The Word on Management, Second Edition
A Topical Index of Scriptures for Managers and Employees
By Mulford, John E. and Winston, Bruce E.
Copyright©1996 Knowledge Elements
ISBN 13: 978-1-62032-542-1
Publication date 8/1/2012
Previously published by JKO Publishing, 1996

Table of Contents

VI. LEADERSHIP CHARACTERISTICS 69

APPENDIX A: MANAGING BY BEATITUDES 71

APPENDIX B: STUDIES IN BUSINESS 111

FOREWORD

The Regent University College of Administration and Management seeks to discover God's truth about business and to communicate that truth to the world. It is with this mission in mind that this reference work began in 1988.

The Bible is a guide for daily life. Yet, many managers and supervisors look past the Bible as a handbook for company policy and personal management style. The Bible was written during a time when computers and rapid transportation were not known. We must understand that men and women have not changed even though technology changed the way we perform certain tasks. The standards of behavior toward God, our employees, our peers and our superiors are still the same. We will not find the words *marketing, information management system, EEOC* and the like in the King James Version, the Revised Standard Version, the New International Version or any other recognized version, but the methods of managing and supervising within these areas are, in fact and principle, contained in Scripture.

The Scriptures refer to workers as *slaves*. Many managers and employees today ignore the passages because slaves are not common in the modern world. However, during the period of time in which the Scriptures were recorded, slaves performed most manual, clerical and household labor. The scriptural references to particular groups of people: *slaves, masters, landowners*, etc. can, today, be substituted with: *employees, supervisors, company owners and CEOs*.

This guide is meant to be a beginning point for Bible study and as a reference. It does not substitute for the study of Scripture. The paraphrases used in this work are designed to interest you, the reader, to continue studying Scripture.

The organizational structure of the text is designed to allow an employee, supervisor or manager to quickly scan major sections and then to find specific areas of concern.

Appendix A is "Managing by Beatitudes." Appendix B is a series of studies by Dr. John E. Mulford, Dean of the School of Business and Mr. Bruce E. Winston, Assistant Professor of Business, which take an intensive look at important business issues of today

I. BUSINESS SYSTEM

The Purpose of Business

Mat. 5:16 Let your light so shine before men, that they may see your good works and give glory to your Father who is in heaven. (RSV)

Rom. 15:5-6 May the God who gives endurance and encouragement give you a spirit of unity among yourselves as you follow Christ Jesus, so that with one heart and mouth you may glorify the God and Father of our Lord Jesus Christ. (NIV)

1 Cor. 10:31 So whether you eat or drink or whatever you do, do it all for the glory of God. (NIV)

2 Thess. 1:11-12 With this in mind, we constantly pray for you, that our God may count you worthy of his calling, and that by his power he may fulfill every good purpose of yours and every act prompted by our faith. We pray this so that the name of our Lord Jesus may be glorified in you, and you in him, according to the grace of our God and the Lord Jesus Christ.

The Practice of Business

Competition

Prov. 24:17-18 Do not rejoice when your enemy falls, and let not your heart be glad when he stumbles; lest the Lord see it, and be displeased, and turn away his anger from him. (RSV)

Prov. 25:21-22 If your enemy is hungry, give him food to eat.

Phil. 3:13-16 Paul tells us to continue toward the goal which is set before us.

Profits

Prov. 14:23 All hard work brings a profit, but mere talk leads only to poverty. (NIV)

Prov. 21:5 The plans of the diligent lead to profit as surely as haste leads to poverty. (NIV)

2 Cor. 9 This chapter discusses sowing and reaping.

Marketing

Prov. 11:26 People curse the man who hordes grain but blessed is the one who is willing to sell. (NIV)

Prov. 20:14 "It's no good, it's no good!" says the buyer; then off he goes and boasts about his purchase. (NIV)

Prov. 27:8 Like a bird that strays from its nest is a man who strays from his home. (Stick to what you're good at.)

Money

Prov. 10:22 The blessing of the Lord brings wealth, and he adds no trouble to it. (NIV)

Eccl. 7:12 Wisdom is a shelter as money is a shelter, but the advantage of knowledge is this: that wisdom preserves the life of its possessor. (NIV)

Eccl. 10:19 A feast is made for laughter, and wine makes life merry, but money is the answer for everything. (NIV)

Interest

Ex. 22:25 If you lend money to the needy... charge no interest.

Lev. 25:36 Do not take interest of any kind from him.

Deut. 23:19 Do not charge your brother interest.

Psalm 15:5 He who lends without usury may live on the Holy hill.

Prov. 28:8 He who increases wealth by exorbitant interest amasses it for another who will be kind to the poor. (NIV)

Ezek. 18:8 He does not lend at usury.

Ezek. 22:12 Jerusalem's sins include usury.

Mat. 25:27; Luke 19:23 In the parable of the talents, the master expected to at least receive his money back from the servant with the interest the bank would have paid.

Lending/Borrowing

Ex. 22:26 If you take a cloak as pledge, return it by sunset.

Deut. 15:8 Freely lend him what he needs.

Deut. 24:6 Do not take a man's livelihood as security for a debt.

Deut. 24:10-12 Let a man bring the pledge to you; do not go and get it. Return a poor man's cloak at night.

Psalm 37:21 The wicked borrow and do not repay.

Psalm 112:5 Good will come to him who lends freely.

Prov. 22:7 ...the borrower is servant to the lender. (NIV)

Ezek. 18:7 Return what is taken in pledge for a loan.

Mat. 5:42 Do not turn away from the one who wants to borrow.

Mat. 6:12 Forgive us our debts as we forgive our debtors.

Rom. 13:8 Let no debt remain outstanding.

Co-signing for a loan

Prov. 6:1-5 If you have put up security for your neighbor, go and plead with your neighbor to free yourself.

Prov. 11:15 He who puts up security for another will surely suffer... (NIV)

Prov. 17:18 A man lacking judgment...puts up security for another. (NIV)

Prov. 22:26-27 Do not pledge security for debts.

Prov. 20:16; Prov. 27:13 If one puts up security for a stranger, take it.

Savings

Prov. 6:8 The ant stores its provisions in summer and gathers its food at harvest.

Prov. 21:20 The wise store choice foods and oil, the fool devours what is stored.

Prov. 30:25 Ants store up food in the summer.

Luke 12:16-21 This parable is about saving up the wrong things.

1 Cor. 16:2 On the first day of every week, each of you should set aside a sum of money in keeping with his income, saving it up… (NIV)

Bankruptcy

Psalm 73:26 My flesh and heart may fail but God is the strength of my heart and my portion forever. (NIV)

Forecasting

James 4:13-15 You do not know what will happen tomorrow.

Foreknowledge

Eccl. 7:14 Therefore a man cannot discover anything about his future.

Eccl. 8:7 No man knows the future, who can tell what is to come?

James 4:13-15 Come now, you who say, "Today or tomorrow we will go into such and such a town and spend a year there and trade and get gain;" whereas you do not know about tomorrow. What is your life? For you are a mist that appears for a little time and then vanishes. Instead you ought to say, "If the Lord wills, we shall live and we shall do this or that." (RSV)

Redistribution of wealth

Psalm 49:10 Wise men die and leave their wealth to others.

Prov. 13:22 A good man leaves an inheritance for his children's children, but a sinner's wealth is stored up for the righteous. (NIV)

Isa. 60:5 ...the wealth of the seas will be brought to you, to you the riches of the nations will come. (NIV)

Zech.14:14 The wealth of all the surrounding nations will be collected.

Forgiveness of debt

Lev. 25:8-10 And thou shalt number seven sabbaths of years unto thee, seven times seven years; and the space of the seven sabbaths of years shall be unto thee forty and nine years. Then shalt thou cause the trumpet of the jubilee to sound on the tenth day of the seventh month, in the day of atonement shall ye make the trumpet sound throughout all your land. And ye shall hallow the fiftieth year, and proclaim liberty throughout all the land unto all the inhabitants thereof: it shall be a jubilee unto you; and ye shall return every man unto his possession, and ye shall return every man unto his family.

Deut. 15:1-3 At the end of every seven years you must cancel debts.

Mat. 6:12 Forgive us our debts as we also forgive our debtors.

Mat. 18:27 The master took pity, canceled his debt and let him go.

Business and Government Relations

Regulation

Rom. 2:25 Do not break the laws.

Taxes

Mat. 22:21; Mark 12:17 Give to Caesar what is Caesar's and to God what is God's.

Luke 3:12-14 Don't collect more tax than you are required to collect.

Authority

Eccl. 5:8-9 Each official is watched by a higher one and others still higher.

Mat. 23:2-3 You must obey the teachers of the law.

Luke 2:1-5 Caesar decreed that a census would be taken.

Rom. 13:1-7 Everyone must submit to the governing authorities.

Tit. 3:1 Remind the people to be subject to rulers and authorities.

1 Pet. 2:13 Submit to every authority instituted among men.

Legal Issues

Prov. 22:22-23 Do not crush the needy in court.

Prov. 22:28; Prov. 23:10-11 Do not move an ancient boundary stone set up by your forefathers. (NIV)

Prov. 25:8-10 Do not rush to go to court, your case may not be as strong as you believe.

Prov. 28:4 Those who forsake the law praise the wicked, but those who keep the law resist them. (NIV)

Prov. 28:5 Evil men do not understand justice... (RSV)

Prov. 28:7 He who keeps the law is a wise son... (RSV)

Prov. 28:9 Turn a deaf ear to the law, and your prayers are detestable. (NIV)

Eccl. 5:5 It is better not to enter into an agreement than to enter into an agreement and not keep it.

Mat. 5:40 ...and if anyone would sue you and take your coat, let him have your cloak as well. (RSV)

Mat. 18:15-17 Discuss the problem with your brother, then with witnesses, then with the church.

Luke 12:58-59 Try to reconcile differences outside of court lest the judge find in favor or your adversary.

1 Cor. 6:1-8 Believers should take their cases before qualified Christians for mediation.

2 Cor. 2:7-8 Now instead you ought to forgive and comfort him.

Wage negotiations

Lev. 19:13 Do not hold back the wages of a hired man.

Eccl. 3:9 What does the worker gain from his toil? (NIV)

Mat. 20:1-15 The parable of the workers in the vineyard. Note that the first two groups of workers agreed to a set wage while the next groups trusted the owner to pay them fairly. Those who contracted for a set wage were the disgruntled group. Each had responsibilities here. The worker has a responsibility to accept what was agreed upon and the owner has a responsibility to pay the workers a living wage.

Mat. 10:10 The worker is worth his keep.

Luke 10:7 The worker deserves his wage.

Rom. 4:4 A man's wages are an obligation and must be paid.

1 Cor. 9:9-11 Do not muzzle an ox while he treads grain.

Col 4:1 Provide your slaves with what is right and fair. (NIV)

1 Tim. 5:18 Do not muzzle an ox and the worker deserves his wage.

2 Tim. 2:6 The farmer should be first to receive a share of the crops.

James 5:4 A cheated workman's cries are heard by God.

Promotions

Prov. 22:29 Do you see a man skilled in his work? He will stand before kings; he will not stand before obscure men. (RSV)

Mat. 25:14-30 The parable of the talents.

Luke 12:42-46 A servant is to be faithful in the master's absence.

Luke 19:12-26 The parable of the ten minas.

Luke 12:48 The person who knows the rules and violates them will be treated more severely than the person who does not know the rules and violates them.

Luke 16:10,12 Whoever can be trusted with very little can also be trusted with much, and whoever is dishonest with very little will also be dishonest with much. So if you have not been trustworthy with someone else's property, who will give you property of your own? (NIV)

1 Cor. 7:17 Retain the place the Lord assigns you.

1 Cor. 7:20 Remain in the situation you were in when God called.

II. WORK FROM THE INDIVIDUAL'S PERSPECTIVE

The Purpose of Work

Prov. 10:4 Lazy hands make a man poor, but diligent hands bring wealth. (NIV)

Prov. 12:11 He who tills his land will have plenty of bread, but he who follows worthless pursuits has no sense. (RSV)

Prov. 14:23 All hard work brings a profit.

Prov. 19:15 Laziness brings on deep sleep.

Prov. 20:4 A sluggard does not plow in the autumn; he will seek at harvest and have nothing. (RSV)

Prov. 22:29 Do you see a man skillful in his work? He will stand before kings; he will not stand before obscure men. (RSV)

Prov. 24:30-34 Laziness and lack of caring will destroy what assets you have. You must wisely use what you have and it will grow more abundant.

Prov. 28:19 Hard work will result in great rewards, worthless pursuits will not yield anything positive.

Eccl. 1:3 What does a man gain from all his labor.

Eccl. 3:13 One of God's gifts to us is that we should be happy and satisfied in our work.

Eccl. 5:12 One who does an honest day's good labor will sleep well. There will be peace in him.

Eccl. 5:18-19 A man should find satisfaction in his labor.

The Practice of Work

Gen. 2:15 God took the man and put him in the Garden of Eden to work.

Gen. 3:17-19 Through painful toil you will eat of it.

Gen. 3:23 God banished him from the Garden of Eden to work the ground.

Ex. 20:9-10 Six days you shall labor and do all your work.

Psalm 90:17 May the favor of the Lord our God rest upon us; establish the work of our hands for us—yes, establish the work of our hands. (NIV)

Eccl. 3:22 "So I saw that there is nothing better for a man than to enjoy his work, because that is his lot. For who can bring him to see what will happen after him?" (NIV)

Eccl. 9:10 In the grave there is neither working nor planning.

Eccl. 10:18 If a man is lazy, the rafters sag; if his hands are idle, the house leaks. (NIV)

John 5:17 "My Father is working still, and I am working." (RSV)

John 17:4 Jesus offers in prayer the idea He has glorified God by completing the work God assigned to him. So also we will glorify God by completing the work He assigns to us.

Acts 20:33-35 These hands of mine have supplied my own needs.

1 Cor. 15:58 Always give yourselves fully to the work of the Lord because you know that your labor in the Lord is not in vain. (NIV)

Eph. 4:28 Let the thief no longer steal, but rather let him labor, doing honest work with his hands, so that he may be able to give to those in need. (RSV)

Col. 3:23 Whatever you do, work at it with all your heart as working for the Lord, not for men. (NIV)

1 Thess. 4:11 Make it your ambition to lead a quiet life, to mind your own business and to work with your hands, just as we told you. (NIV)

2 Thess. 3:10 If a person who is able to work and to contribute won't help, then he should not eat.

Submission to authority

Prov. 27:18 He who tends a fig tree will eat its fruit, and he who guards his master will be honored. (RSV)

Eccl. 8:2-5 Obey the king's command, even if the task is unpleasant.

Eccl. 10:20 Do not revile the king even in your thoughts, or curse the rich in your bedroom, because a bird of the air may carry your words, and a bird on the wing may report what you say. (NIV)

Mat. 8:8-9; *Luke 7:7-8* The centurion understood authority and orders. He was under authority and had authority over other men.

Eph. 6:5-9 Slaves, (employees) obey your earthly masters with respect.

Tit. 3:1 Remind the people to be subject to rulers and authorities.

1 Pet. 2:18 Slaves, submit yourselves to your masters with all respect, not only to those who are good and considerate, but also to those who are harsh.

Obedience to Authority

Luke 12:42-48 The parable of watchfulness.

Rom. 13:1-2 Everyone must submit himself to the governing authorities, for there is no authority except that which God has established. The authorities that exist have been established by God. (NIV)

1 Pet. 2:13-14 Be subject for the Lord's sake to every human institution, whether it be to the emperor as supreme, or to governors as sent by him to punish those who do wrong and to praise those who do right. (RSV)

III. ETHICAL ISSUES IN BUSINESS

Personal Ethics

Tithe

Ex. 23:19 Bring the best of your first fruits to the house of God.

Lev. 27:30 A tithe of everything belongs to the Lord.

Deut. 14:22 Set aside a tenth of all your field's produce each year.

1 Chron. 29:14 Who are we to give as this? All comes from God. (NIV)

Prov. 3:9 Honor the Lord with your wealth, with the first fruits of your crops. (NIV)

Mal. 3:10 Bring the whole tithe in to the storehouse and God will bless you more than you have room.

Mat. 10:8 Freely you have received, freely give.

Mark 12:41-44; Luke 21:1-4 The story of the widow's mite.

Luke 6:38 Give and it will be given to you.

Alms

Prov. 11:24-25 One man gives freely, yet gains more; another withholds unduly, but comes to poverty. (NIV)

Prov. 14:21 …happy is he who is kind to the needy. (RSV)

Prov. 19:17 He who is kind to the poor lends to the Lord, and he will repay him for his deed. (RSV)

Prov. 21:13 If you don't hear the poor, the Lord won't answer you.

Prov. 22:9 A generous man will be blessed.

Prov. 28:27 He who gives to the poor will lack nothing,… (NIV)

Luke 11:41 Give what is inside the dish to the poor.

Luke 12:33 Sell your possessions and give to the poor.

Acts 2:45 They gave to anyone who had need.

Acts 4:32-37 The members of the early new testament church shared everything they had.

Acts 10:2 …he gave generously to those in need.

Rom. 12:13 Share with God's people who are in need. Practice hospitality. (NIV)

Corporate Ethics

Honesty

Lev. 19:35-36 God commands the Israelites to use honest measurements for length, weight or quantity. The Old Testament contains many references to honest scales and measures. Today, managers and employees do not carry scales with them. Rather examine the scriptures referenced here and substitute time clocks, mileage allowances, expense account reports, carton counts reported on manifests, quality control counts for the scales and weights used by the Old Testament merchants.

Deut. 25:13-15 Do not have two differing weights in your bag.

Prov. 14:5 A truthful witness does not deceive, but a false witness pours out lies. (NIV)

Prov. 16:11 Honest scales and balances are from the Lord; all the weights in the bag are of his making. (NIV)

Prov. 16:13 Kings take pleasure in honest lips; they value a man who speaks the truth. (NIV)

Prov. 19:5 A false witness will not go unpunished, and he who utters lies will not escape. (RSV)

Prov. 20:10 Differing weights and measures, the Lord detests them both. (NIV)

Prov. 20:23 The Lord detests differing weights, and dishonest scales do not please him. (NIV)

Prov. 21:6 A fortune made by a lying tongue is a fleeting vapor and a deadly snare. (NIV)

Prov. 21:28 A false witness will perish.

Prov. 25:18 A man who bears false witness against his neighbor is like a war club, or a sword, or a sharp arrow. (RSV)

Prov. 29:27 The righteous detest the dishonest; the wicked detest the upright. (NIV)

2 Cor. 13:8 For we cannot do anything against the truth, but only for truth. (RSV)

Stealing

Lev. 19:11 Do not steal.

Prov. 29:24 The accomplice of a thief is his own enemy; he is put under oath and dare not testify. (NIV)

Eph. 4:28 Let the thief no longer steal, but rather let him labor, doing honest work with his hands, so that he may be able to give to those in need. (RSV)

Integrity

Job 2:3 God praised Job because Job maintained his integrity even when he was mistreated and suffering greatly.

Job 31:6 Let me be weighed in a just balance, and let God know my integrity! (RSV)

Psalms 25:21 May integrity and uprightness protect me for my hope is in You. (NIV)

Prov. 11:3 The integrity of the upright shall guide them... (KJV)

Prov. 17:23 A wicked man accepts a bribe in secret to pervert the course of justice. (NIV)

Prov. 17:26 To impose a fine on a righteous man is not good; to flog noble men is wrong. (RSV)

Prov. 20:11 Even a child is known by his actions, by whether his conduct is pure and right. (NIV)

Prov. 21:3 To do what is right and just is more acceptable to the Lord... (NIV)

Prov. 25:13 Like the coolness of snow at harvest time is a trustworthy messenger to those who send him; he refreshes the spirit of his masters. (NIV)

Eccl. 7:7 ...a bribe corrupts the heart.

Mat. 5:37 Simply let your yes be a yes and your no be a no.

Mat. 7:12 Treat everyone as you desire them to treat you.

Mat. 21:28-31 The parable of the two sons.

Eph. 5:3-5 But among you there must not be even a hint of sexual immorality, or of any kind of impurity, or of greed, because these are improper for God's holy people. Nor should there be obscenity, foolish talk or coarse joking, which are out of place, but rather thanksgiving. For of this you can be sure: no immoral, impure or greedy person—such a man is an idolater—has any inheritance in the kingdom of Christ and of God. (NIV)

2 Tim. 3:1-7 In the last days, men will lose their integrity and become lovers of things which God abhors.

Tit. 2:7-8 In everything, set them an example by doing what is good. In your teaching show integrity, seriousness and soundness of speech that cannot be condemned, so that those who oppose you may be ashamed because they have nothing bad to say about you. (NIV)

Greed

Ex. 20:17; Deut. 5:21 You shall not covet.

Prov. 11:4 Wealth is worthless in the day of wrath. (NIV)

Prov. 15:27 A greedy man brings trouble to his family. (NIV)

Prov. 28:22 A stingy man is eager to get rich and is unaware that poverty awaits him. (NIV)

Prov. 28:25 A greedy man stirs up strife. (RSV)

Eccl. 4:4 Then I saw that all toil and all skill in work come from a man's envy of his neighbor. This also is vanity and a striving after wind. (RSV)

Mat. 6:19 We should not be concerned about building up treasures here on earth, but rather about the more meaningful treasures of everlasting life.

Mark 8:36 If a person gains all the material wealth, the largest office or buildings but loses his soul in the process, did he really gain anything significant? Was it worth dying for?

Luke 12:15 Greed is all around us, we are to be on guard against it at all times.

1 Cor. 5:11 You must not associate with anyone who calls himself a brother but is…greedy… (NIV)

1 Tim. 6:10 For the love of money is the root of all evils… (RSV)

Heb. 13:5 Keep your lives free from the love of money.

Confidentiality

Neh. 2:12 I had not told anyone what my God had put in my heart to do. (NIV)

Prov. 20:19 A gossip betrays a confidence.

Prov. 21:23 He who guards his mouth and his tongue, keeps himself from calamity. (NIV)

Prov. 25:2 It is the glory of God to conceal a matter; to search out a matter is the glory of kings. (NIV)

Trustworthiness

Num. 30:2 If a man has made a promise, he must not break his word.

Jer. 13:20 Where is the flock that was entrusted to you, the sheep of which you boasted? (NIV)

Mat. 5:37 Simply let your yes be yes and your no, no.

Luke 16:12 If you have not been trustworthy with someone else's property, who will give you property of your own? (NIV)

1 Cor. 4:1-2 We ought to be regarded as servants of Christ and stewards of the mysteries of God. It is necessary that those who have been given a trust be faithful.

1 Tim. 6:20 O Timothy, guard what has been entrusted to you. (RSV)

James 5:12 Let your yes be yes, and no, no or you will be condemned.

Deception

Prov. 6:12-14 The characteristics of a villain are lying, signaling with his hands, stirring up trouble among people and planning evil things. Calamity will suddenly overthrow him.

Prov. 24:28 Be not a witness against your neighbor without cause, and do not deceive with your lips. (RSV)

Prov. 28:13 He who conceals his sins does not prosper, but whoever confesses and renounces them finds mercy. (NIV)

Jer. 37:9 The Lord says we should not deceive ourselves.

Mat. 24:4 Jesus admonished the disciples to be careful and not let anyone lead them astray.

Rom. 16:18 Paul warns the followers in Rome to be wary of people who cause division among the church and disagree with the teaching. By smooth talk and flattery they deceive the minds of naive people. (NIV)

1 Cor. 3:18 Let no one deceive himself. If any one of you thinks he is wise in this age, let him become a fool that he may become wise. (RSV)

2 Cor. 4:2 As Christians we should not use deception.

Eph. 5:6 Let no one deceive you with empty words, for it is because of these things that the wrath of God comes upon the sons of diso-bedience. (RSV)

Conflict of Interest

Prov. 17:8 A bribe (gift) is a charm to the one who gives it; wherever he turns, he succeeds. (NIV)

Prov. 17:23 A wicked man accepts a bribe in secret to pervert the course of justice. (NIV)

Prov. 18:16 A gift opens the way for the giver and ushers him into the presence of the great. (NIV)

Luke 16:13 No servant can serve two masters. Either he will hate the one and love the other, or he will be devoted to the one and despise the other. (NIV)

Rom. 7:23 But I see another law at work in the members of my body, waging war against the law of my mind and making me a prisoner of the law of sin at work within my members. (NIV)

1 Cor. 10:24 Nobody should seek his own good, but the good of others. (NIV)

Phil. 2:4 Let each of you look not only to his own interests, but also to the interests of others. (RSV)

1 Thess. 5:22 Avoid every kind of evil. (NIV)

Heb. 13:5 ...be content with what you have.

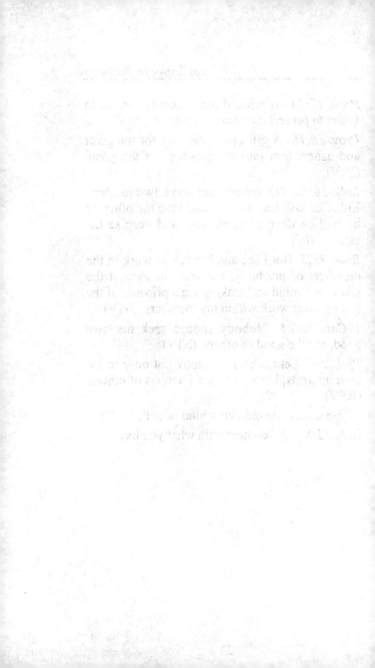

IV. INTERPERSONAL RELATIONS

Attitudes

Servanthood

Gen. 12-14 God told Abraham to leave all he had and move. In chapter 14, Abraham takes from the king of Sodom only what his men had eaten. He was not concerned for his own wealth.

Mat. 20:25-28; Mark 10:42-45 Whoever wants to become great must be your servant.

Mark 9:35 If anyone wants to be first, he must be the very last...

Luke 9:48 For he who is least among you, he is the greatest.

Luke 13:30 Those who are last will be first, and the first will be last.

Luke 14:8-11 When looking for a place to sit or deciding where in a group you should be take the lowest place so when the host (or supervisor) comes he might move you up to a better place.

Luke 22:25-27 The greatest among you should be the youngest.

John 13:4-17 Jesus washes the feet of the disciples as an example of servitude.

Acts 6:1-5 The people chose leaders (deacons) who would serve the people.

Phil. 2:4 Look toward the interest of others.

The Authority of God

Gen. 1:1 In the beginning God created…

Deut. 10:14 To the Lord your God belong the heavens,…

1 Chron. 29:12 Wealth and honor come from you — you are the ruler of all things. (NIV)

Job 1:21 Job accepted the fact that all things come from God, that all things belong to God, and that all things return to God. God will choose how long we are to have something.

Psalm 24:1 The earth is the Lord's and everything in it.

Psalm 50:10 God said "for every animal is mine, the cattle on a thousand hills."

Psalm 100:3 God made us and we are his.

Haggai 2:8 The silver is mine, and the gold is mine says the Lord of hosts. (RSV)

Mat. 28:18 All authority in heaven and on earth has been given to me. (RSV)

John 1:1 In the beginning was the Word and the Word was with God, and the Word was God. (RSV)

John 1:3 Through Him all things were made; without him nothing was made that has been made. (NIV)

Acts 17:24 God made the world and everything in it.

Rom. 11:36 For from Him and through Him and to Him are all things. (RSV)

Col. 1:16-17 For by Him all things were created.

Submission to God

Deut. 8:17-18 It is He who gives you the ability to produce wealth.

Psalm 24:1 The earth is the Lord's and everything in it. (NIV) (This includes all of the company's resources and people.)

Psalm 119 This Psalm provides the manager a prayer from which all other activities will be focused. The Psalmist writes about focusing our eyes on God's law, living God's way, trusting in God through difficulties, God's unchanging law and His love for us.

Prov. 18:10 The name of the Lord is a strong tower; the righteous run to it. (NIV)

Prov. 20:27 The lamp of the Lord searches the spirit of a man; it searches out his inmost being. (NIV)

Prov. 21:1 The king's heart is in the hand of the Lord; he directs it like a watercourse wherever he pleases. (NIV)

Prov. 22:2 Rich and poor have this in common, the Lord is the maker of them all. (NIV)

Prov. 28:14 Blessed is the man who fears the Lord always… (RSV)

Prov. 29:13 The poor man and the oppressor have this in common; the Lord gives sight to the eyes of both. (NIV)

Prov. 30:5 Every word of God proves true; he is a shield to those who take refuge in him. (RSV)

Eccl. 9:1 The righteous and the wise and what they do are in God's hands.

Eccl. 12:13-14 Fear God and keep his commandments for God will bring every deed into judgment.

Isa. 2:8-9 Man will be brought down for worshipping idols.

Mat. 1:19-24 Joseph did what the angel of the Lord commanded.

Mat. 3:13-15 Jesus said "Let it be so to fulfill all righteousness."

Mat. 21:12-13; Mark 11:15-17; Luke 19:45-46; John 2:13-17 Jesus overturns the money-changers' tables.

Luke 1:31-38 Mary was obedient to the will of God.

Luke 16:13 No one can serve two masters...

John 19:10-11 Jesus tells Pilate that Pilate has no power except what God has given him.

Acts 4:18-19 Peter obeys God rather than man.

Acts 9:10-19 Ananias obeys God though he is cautious about Saul.

Acts 12:21-23 Herod did not give praise to God, and an angel struck him down.

Submission to authority

Prov. 27:18 He who tends a fig tree will eat its fruit, and he who guards his master will be honored. (RSV)

Eccl. 8:2-5 Obey the king's command, even if the task is unpleasant.

Eccl. 10:20 Do not revile the king even in your thoughts, or curse the rich in your bedroom, because a bird of the air may carry your words, and a bird on the wing may report what you say. (NIV)

Mat. 8:8-9; Luke 7:7-8 The centurion understood authority and orders. He was under authority and had authority over other men.

Eph. 6:5-9 Slaves, (employees) obey your earthly masters with respect.

Tit. 3:1 Remind the people to be subject to rulers and authorities.

1 Pet. 2:18 Slaves, submit yourselves to your masters with all respect, not only to those who are good and considerate, but also to those who are harsh.

Obedience to God

Prov. 21:30 There is no wisdom, no insight, no plan that can succeed against the Lord. (NIV)

Mat. 24:45-47 Keep obedience; we don't know when our Lord returns.

Mat. 26:39 "Yet not as I will, but as you will."

Mark 14:36 "Yet not what I will, but what you will."

Luke 5:5 …But because you say so, I will let down the nets. (NIV)

Luke 22:42 "Yet not my will but yours be done."

John 14:31 …but I do as the Father has commanded me. (RSV)

Acts 9:10-18 Ananias obeys God though he distrusts Saul.

Obedience to authority

Luke 12:42-48 The parable of watchfulness.

Rom. 13:1-2 Everyone must submit himself to the governing authorities, for there is no authority except that which God has established. The authorities that exist have been established by God. (NIV)

1 Pet. 2:13-14 Be subject for the Lord's sake to every human institution, whether it be to the emperor as supreme, or to governors as sent by him to punish those who do wrong and to praise those who do right. (RSV)

Goal-orientation

Prov. 16:26 The laborer's appetite works for him; his hunger drives him on. (NIV)

1 Cor. 9:24-27 Do you not know that in a race all the runners run, but only one gets the prize: Run in such a way as to get the prize. Everyone who competes in the games goes into strict training. They do it to get a crown that will not last; but we do it to get a crown that will last forever. Therefore I do not run like a man running aimlessly; I do not fight like a man beating the air. No, I beat my body and make it my slave so that after I have preached to others, I myself will not be disqualified for the prize. (NIV)

Relationships

Prov. 12:26 A righteous man is cautious in friendship,... (NIV)

Prov. 16:28 Gossip separates close friends.

Prov. 17:14 Starting a quarrel is like breaching a dam, so drop the matter before a dispute breaks out. (NIV)

Mat. 7:12; Luke 6:31 In everything, do to others what you would have them do to you.

Mat. 9:10-12; Mark 2:15-17 Jesus associates with sinners and tax collectors.

Mat. 22:39; Mark 12:28-31 Love your neighbor as yourself.

1 Cor. 10:24 Nobody should seek his own good, but the good of others. (NIV)

1 Cor. 15:33 Do not be misled: Bad company corrupts good character. (NIV)

Stewardship

Mat. 21:33-41 The parable of the talents.

Mark 12:1-11 The parable of the tenants.

Rom. 12:6-8 Let each use his gifts.

Judging

Deut. 1:17 Do not show partiality in judging, hear both great and small alike. (NIV)

Deut. 19:15 A single witness shall not prevail against a man for any crime or for any wrong in connection with any offense that he has committed; only on the evidence of two witnesses, or of three witnesses, shall a charge be sustained. (RSV)

1 Kings 8:31-32 ...condemn the guilty and declare the innocent not guilty.

Prov. 12:11 He who chases fantasy lacks judgment. (NIV)

Prov. 20:8 When a king sits on his throne to judge, he winnows out all evil with his eyes. (NIV)

Prov. 24:23-25 To show partiality in judging is not good.

Prov. 28:16 A tyrannical ruler lacks judgment.

Prov. 28:21 To show partiality is not good.

Prov. 29:4 By justice a king gives a country stability.

Prov. 29:14 If a king judges the poor with equity, his throne will always be established forever. (RSV)

Prov. 29:26 Many seek the favor of a ruler, but from the Lord a man gets justice.

Luke 6:37 Do not judge and you will not be judged.

Forgiveness

1 Kings 8:46-50 …if they repent and plead with you…forgive all the offenses. (NIV)

Psalm 32:1 Blessed is he whose transgressions are forgiven.

Psalm 130:3-4 But with you there is forgiveness, therefore you are feared.

Micah 7:18 Who is a God like you, who pardons sin and forgives?

Mat. 5:39 If some one strikes you on the right cheek, turn the other also.

Mat. 6:14-15 If you forgive men...your Father will also forgive you.

Mat. 6:12 Forgive us our debts.

Mat. 7:3-4 Why do you look at the speck in your brother's eye and pay no attention to the plank in your own? (NIV)

Mat. 18:21-22 How often shall we forgive our brother?

Mark 11:25 And whenever you stand praying, forgive, if you have anything against anyone; so that your Father also who is in heaven may forgive you your trespasses. (RSV)

Luke 11:4 Forgive us our sins for we also forgive everyone who is indebted to us. (RSV)

Luke 17:3-4 ...if he repents forgive him...

Luke 23:34 Jesus asks for forgiveness from God for what the people have done to him.

John 20:23 If you forgive the sins of any, they are forgiven; if you retain the sins of any, they are retained. (RSV)

Acts 2:38 Repent and be baptized...for the forgiveness of your sins.

Acts 8:22 Perhaps he will forgive you for having such thoughts in your heart. (NIV)

Acts 13:38 ...through Jesus the forgiveness of sins is proclaimed to you. (NIV)

Rom. 4:7-8 Blessed are they whose transgressions are forgiven.

2 Cor. 2:7-8 Now instead you ought to forgive and comfort him... (NIV)

Eph. 4:32 And be kind to one another, tender-hearted, forgiving one another, as God in Christ forgave you. (RSV)

Col. 3:13 Forgive whatever grievances you may have against one another.

James 5:15-16 If he has sinned, he will be forgiven.

1 John 1:9 If we confess our sins, he is faithful and just and will forgive us... (NIV)

Humility/Pride

2 Kings 22:19 "...you humbled yourselves...I heard you," declares the Lord.

2 Chron. 7:14 If my people will humble themselves, I will hear from heaven.

Psalms 18:27 You save the humble but bring low those whose eyes are haughty. (NIV)

Prov. 3:34 He mocks proud mockers but gives grace to the humble. (NIV)

Prov. 11:2 When pride comes, then comes disgrace, but with humility comes wisdom. (NIV)

Prov. 12:9 Better to be a nobody and yet have a servant than pretend to be somebody and have no food. (NIV)

Prov. 16:18 Pride goes before destruction, and a haughty spirit before a fall. (RSV)

Prov. 18:12 Before his downfall a man's heart is proud, but humility comes before honor. (NIV)

Prov. 22:4 Humility and the fear of the Lord bring wealth and honor and life. (NIV)

Prov. 29:23 A man's pride will bring him low, but he who is lowly in spirit will obtain honor. (RSV)

Zeph. 2:3 Seek the Lord, all you humble of the land, do what he commands. (NIV)

Mat. 18:4 Whoever humbles himself like this child, he is the greatest in the Kingdom of heaven. (RSV)

Mat. 23:12 Whoever exalts himself will be humbled, and whoever humbles himself will be exalted. (RSV)

Luke 14:11 For everyone who exalts himself will be humbled, and he who humbles himself will be exalted. (RSV)

Luke 18:14 ...For everyone who exalts himself will be humbled, and he who humbles himself will be exalted. (NIV)

Acts 20:19 Paul served the Lord with great humility and with tears.

Gal. 5:26 Let us not become conceited, provoking and envying each other. (NIV)

Phil. 2:3-4 Do nothing from selfishness or conceit, but in humility count others better than yourselves. Let each of you look not only to his own interest, but also to the interest of others. (RSV)

James 4:6 God opposes the proud but gives grace to the humble. (RSV)

James 4:10 Humble yourselves before the Lord, and he will exalt you. (RSV)

1 Pet. 5:5-6 God opposes the proud but gives grace to the humble. (Peter is quoting from Proverbs.)

Materialism

Prov. 11:4 Wealth is worthless in the day of wrath. (NIV)

Prov. 13:11 Wealth hastily gotten will dwindle, but he who gathers little by little will increase it. (RSV)

Prov. 23:4 Do not wear yourself out to get rich; have the wisdom to show restraint. (NIV)

Mat. 6:19 Do not store treasure on earth but in heaven.

Mat. 16:26 What good will it be for a man if he gains the whole world but loses his soul? (NIV)

Mark 8:36 What good is it for a man to gain the whole world, yet forfeit his soul. (NIV)

Luke 12:16-21 The parable of the rich man and the barns.

Luke 12:33-34 ...a treasure in heaven that will not wear out... For where your treasure is, there your heart will be also.

Heb. 13:5 Keep your lives free from the love of money.

Retaliation

Lev. 19:18 Do not seek revenge or bear a grudge against one of your people, but love your neighbor as yourself. (NIV)

Prov. 17:9 He who covers over an offense promotes love, but whoever repeats the matter separates close friends. (NIV)

Prov. 17:13 If a man returns evil for good, evil will not depart from his house. (RSV)

Prov. 20:22 Do not say, "I'll pay you back." Wait for the Lord to help you.

Prov. 24:29 Do not say, "I'll do to him as he has done to me..."

Mat. 5:38-39 If someone strikes you on the right cheek, turn the other also.

Mat. 5:43-44 Love your enemies and pray for those who persecute you.

Mat. 12:25 A kingdom divided cannot stand.

Rom. 12:17-19 Do not repay anyone evil for evil.

Gal. 5:15 If you keep on biting and devouring each other, watch out, or you will be destroyed by each other. (NIV)

Col. 3:13 Forgive each other as the Lord forgave you.

Kindness

Prov. 11:16-17 A kindhearted woman gains respect... a kind man benefits himself. (NIV)

Patience

Psalm 27:14 Wait for the Lord: be strong and take heart and wait for the Lord. (NIV)

Psalm 37:7 Be still before the Lord and wait patiently for him... (RSV)

Psalm 40:1 I waited patiently for the Lord; He turned to me and heard my cry. (NIV)

Prov. 14:29 A patient man has great understanding… (NIV)

Prov. 16:32 Better a patient man than a warrior … (NIV)

Prov. 19:11 A man's wisdom gives him patience; it is his glory to overlook an offense.

Prov. 25:15 With patience a ruler may be persuaded,… (RSV)

Eccl. 7:8 …and patience is better than pride. (NIV)

Rom. 8:25 If we hope for what we do not yet have, we wait for it patiently. (NIV)

Rom. 12:12 Be patient in difficulties.

1 Cor. 13:4 Love is patient.

Gal. 5:22 One of the fruits of the spirit is patience.

Gal. 6:9 Don't tire in your efforts; in time you will see the results.

Eph. 4:2 Be patient.

Col. 1:11 Pray for patience, so you will be able to endure patiently and with joy.

Money

Prov. 13:11 Dishonest money dwindles away, but he who gathers money little by little makes it grow. (NIV)

Prov. 23:4 Do not wear yourself out to get rich; have the wisdom to show restraint. (NIV)

Eccl. 5:10 Whoever loves money never has money enough; whoever loves wealth is never satisfied with his income. This too is meaningless. (NIV).

Mat. 6:19-21 Store up treasure in heaven, not on earth.

Mat. 25:14-30 The parable of the talents.

1 Cor. 16:2 On the first day of every week, each of you should set aside a sum of money in keeping with his income, saving it up... (NIV)

1 Tim. 6:10 The love of money is the root of all kinds of evil. (RSV)

1 Tim. 6:17 Command the rich not to hope in wealth, but in God.

Heb. 13:5 Keep your lives free from the love of money.

Justice

Ex. 23:7 Have nothing to do with a false charge.

Lev. 5:1 If a person...does not speak up regarding something he has seen or learned, he will be held responsible. (NIV)

Deut. 16:19 Do not pervert justice or show partiality. Do not accept a bribe, for a bribe blinds the eyes of the wise and twists the words of the righteous. (NIV)

Deut. 24:17 We must watch over the homeless, the weak and visitors and insure they receive justice.

Psalm 106:3 Blessed are they who observe justice, who do righteousness at all times! (RSV)

Prov. 29:26 Many seek an audience with a ruler, but it is from the Lord that man gets justice. (NIV)

Eccl. 5:8 If you see...rights and justice denied...do not be surprised. (NIV)

Isa. 1:17 Learn to do good, seek justice... (RSV)

Isa. 56:1 Maintain justice and do what is right. (NIV)

Isa. 61:8 For I, the Lord, love justice, I hate robbery and wrong... (RSV)

Luke 11:42 Woe to you Pharisees...you neglect justice. (NIV)

Luke 18:1-5 The parable of the persistent widow.

Luke 23:41 We are punished justly, we are getting what our deeds deserve.

Col. 4:1 Masters, treat your slaves justly and fairly, knowing that you also have a Master in heaven. (RSV)

Heb. 11:33 Who through faith conquered kingdoms, enforced justice. (RSV)

Authority

2 Sam. 23:3-4 When one rules over men in righteousness, when he rules in the fear of God, he is like the light of morning at sunrise. (NIV)

Eccl. 8:9 There is a time when a man lords it over others to his own hurt. (NIV)

Mat. 8:8-9 The centurion who is under authority and has authority understands the authority of

Jesus and recognizes how Jesus can command and it will be done.

Mat. 20:25-28 The gentile rulers abuse authority and lord their position over people.

Luke 7:8 For I myself am a man under authority, with soldiers under me.

1 Pet. 5:2-3 Be shepherds of God's flock that is under your care, serving as overseers—not because you must, but because you are willing, as God wants you to be; not greedy for money, but eager to serve; not lording it over those entrusted to you, but being examples to the flock. (NIV)

Accountability

Mat. 5:13-16 If the salt loses its saltiness, how can it be made salty again?

Mat. 25:14-30 The parable of the talents.

Luke 12:47-48 If someone does not know the rules and regulations and violates the rules, he will be punished less than the one who knew the rules and regulations yet still broke them. (Having knowledge increases our accountability.)

Luke 16:1-2 The parable of the shrewd manager.

Rom. 12:17-18 Do not repay evil with evil, do what is right in the eyes of everybody. (NIV) (We are accountable even to those to whom our actions are directed.)

1 Cor. 4:2 Moreover it is required of stewards that they be found trustworthy. (RSV)

Conflict Management

Eccl. 10:4 If a ruler's anger rises against you, do not leave your post; calmness can lay great errors to rest. (NIV) (If you find yourself in an argument with your superior, do not walk off the job. Remain calm and schedule a time later in the day to continue the discussion.)

Mat. 5:9 Blessed are the peacemakers, they will be called the sons of God. (RSV)

Mat. 5:23-26 First go and be reconciled with your brother, then offer...

Mat. 12:25 A kingdom divided can not stand.

Mat. 18:15-17 If your brother sins against you, go and tell him his fault, between you and him alone. If he listens to you, you have gained your brother. (RSV)

Acts 15:36-41 Paul's and Barnabas' unresolved conflict led to separation. Together, how much more could they have accomplished for God?

Rom. 12:18 As far as possible, live at peace with one another.

1 Cor. 6:1-8 Paul admonishes Christians not to take our conflicts before the ungodly to seek resolution.

Phil. 2:4 Look toward the interests of others.

Col. 3:13 Bear with one another and forgive.

James 5:16 Confess your sins to one another...the prayer of a righteous man is powerful and effective. (NIV) (Discuss your problems and transgressions with another person. There is wisdom in advice, and the prayers of two are strong.)

Skills

Listening

Prov. 1:5 Wise people will listen and learn more.

Prov. 4:1 Listen, my sons, to a father's instruction; pay attention and gain understanding. (NIV)

Prov. 4:20 Pay attention to what I say; listen closely to my words. (NIV)

Prov. 7:24 Now then, my sons, listen to me; pay attention to what I say. (NIV)

Prov. 18:13 Answering before listening is ridiculous and shameful.

Neh. 1:11 O Lord, let your ear be attentive to your servant. (NIV)

Heb. 2:1 We must pay careful attention to what we hear.

James 1:19 Be quick to listen, slow to speak and slow to anger.

Stress

Psalm 23:4 Though I walk through the valley of death, I will fear no evil.

Psalm 25:15 My eyes are ever on the Lord, for only he will release my feet from the snare. (NIV)

Psalm 27:1-2 The Lord is my light...whom shall I fear? (NIV)

Psalm 34:4 I sought the Lord and ... he delivered me from my fears. (NIV)

Psalm 34:19 Many are the afflictions of the righteous; but the Lord delivers him out of them all. (RSV)

Psalm 56:3-4 When I am afraid I will trust in You.

Psalm 94:19 When anxiety was great within me your consolation brought joy to my soul. (NIV)

Psalm 119:50,93 My comfort in my suffering is this: your promise renews my life. I will never forget your precepts, for by them you have renewed my life. (NIV)

Psalm 139:23 Search me, O God, know my heart; test me and know my anxious thoughts. (NIV)

Prov. 12:25 Anxiety in a man's heart weighs him down, but a good word makes him glad. (RSV)

Prov. 24:10 If you falter in times of trouble, how small is your strength. (NIV)

Prov. 24:19-20 Do not fret because of evil men, for they have no future.

Eccl. 7:10 Do not say, "Why were the old days better than these?" For it is not wise to ask such questions. (NIV)

Eccl. 10:4 If a ruler's anger rises against you, do not leave your post; calmness can lay great errors to rest. (NIV)

Isa. 41:10 Fear not, for I am with you, be not dismayed, for I am your God: I will strengthen you, I will help you, I will uphold you with my victorious right hand. (RSV)

Mat. 6:34 Therefore do not be anxious about tomorrow, for tomorrow will be anxious for itself. Let the day's own trouble be sufficient for the day. (RSV)

Luke 12:22-31 Therefore I tell you, do not worry about your life... (RSV) (Jesus taught about anxiety. His teaching on anxiety concludes with 'Instead, seek his kingdom, and these things shall be yours as well.' (RSV)

Rom. 5:3-5 We know that suffering produces perseverance, perseverance builds character and character builds hope...

2 Cor. 1:3-5 God comforts us in all of our troubles.

2 Cor. 12:9-10 ...My grace is sufficient for you, for my power is made perfect in weakness, I will all the more gladly boast of my weaknesses, that the power of Christ may rest upon me. For the sake of Christ, then, I am content with weaknesses, insults, hardships, persecutions, and calamities; for when I am weak, then I am strong. (RSV)

Eph. 6:10-12 Be strong in the Lord and in his mighty power.

Phil. 4:6-7 Have no anxiety about anything, but in everything by prayer and supplication with thanksgiving let your requests be made known to God and the peace of God, which passes all understanding, will keep your hearts and your minds in Christ Jesus. (RSV)

1 Thess. 5:16-18 Paul admonishes the Thessalonians to give thanks to God regardless of what happens, for all things are the will of God.

Heb. 13:6 The Lord is my helper, I will not be afraid.

James 1:2 Consider it joy, when you face trials of many kinds.

James 5:11 ...consider blessed those who have persevered... (NIV)

1 Pet. 1:6 In this you rejoice now, you may have had to suffer grief in all trials. (RSV)

1 Pet. 5:7 Cast all your anxiety on him for he cares about you. (RSV)

Time Management

Prov. 6:10-11 A little sleep, a little slumber, a little folding of the hands to rest—and poverty will come on you like a bandit. (NIV)

Prov. 24:27 Finish your outdoor work and get your fields ready; after that finish your house. (NIV)

Eccl. 3:1-8 There is a time for everything.

Eccl. 3:17 There is a time for every activity and deed.

Mat. 26:45 Jesus chastises the disciples for sleeping and not watching.

Self-Confidence

Ex. 14:13-14 Do not be afraid, stand firm and ...the deliverance of the Lord will bring you through.

Joshua 2:24 The Lord has given you the world.

Joshua 8:1 The Lord told Joshua, "So be not afraid, do not be discouraged."

Prov. 3:26 For the Lord will be your confidence and will keep your foot from being snared. (NIV)

Mat. 10:31 So don't be afraid; you are worth many sparrows.

Mark 5:36 Ignoring what they said, Jesus told the synagogue ruler, "Don't be afraid; just believe." (NIV)

Luke 12:32 "Fear not, little flock, for it is your Father's good pleasure to give you the kingdom." (RSV)

1 Tim. 4:12 Don't let any one look down on you because you are young, but set an example for the believers in speech, in life, in love, in faith and in purity. (NIV)

Heb. 13:6 The Lord is my helper, I will not be afraid.

Self-Control

Prov. 23:20-21 Do not join drunkards and gluttons for you should not surround yourself with what is not good.

Prov. 25:28 A man without self control is like a city broken into and left without walls. (RSV)

Prov. 29:11 A wise man keeps himself under self-control.

Dan. 10:2-3 Daniel fasted for three weeks.

Rom. 6:12-13 Do not let sin reign in your mortal body.

Gal. 5:24 Those who belong to Christ Jesus have crucified the sinful nature with its passions and desires.

Eph. 4:22 Put off your old self, which is corrupted by its deceitful desires.

Col. 3:5-10 Put to death whatever belongs to your earthly nature...

1 Pet. 2:11-12 Live good lives among the pagans that...they glorify God...

1 Pet. 4:2-3 Live not for earthly desires, but for the will of God.

1 Pet. 5:8 Be self-controlled and alert.

Family

Gen. 2:24 For this reason a man will leave his father and mother and be united to his wife, and they will become one flesh. (NIV)

Psalm 127 This psalm admonishes Solomon to pay more attention to his sons and family than he has been. He had focused his attention on his work and accomplishments.

Prov. 5:15-23 The writer of these proverbs admonishes the husband to remember the responsibilities of marriage and the importance of fidelity. With responsibility comes joy.

Prov. 11:29 He who brings trouble on his family will inherit only wind.

Prov. 19:18 Discipline your son while there is hope; do not set your heart on his destruction. (RSV)

Prov. 22:6 Train up a child in the way he should go, and when he is old he will not depart from it. (RSV)

Luke 2:51 Jesus was obedient to his parents.

1 Cor. 7 Paul discusses marriage and the responsibilities in marriage.

Col. 3:18-25 The relationship of family members and there interactions are presented by Paul. Each has responsibilities to the others.

Delegation

Num. 27:18-21 Moses gives authority to Joshua as commanded by God.

Neh. 7:2 Nehemiah put Hanani in charge.

Prov. 13:13 He who respects a command is rewarded.

Mat. 25:14-30 The parable of the talents.

Acts 13:2-3 God sets Barnabas and Saul apart for work.

1 Cor. 3:6 Paul planted, Apollos watered, and God made it grow.

Functional Gifts

(These passages on functional gifts carry a central theme. Each person has specific skills and traits which uniquely equip them to perform a specific function within the organization. Each must serve the greater organization cheerfully and, at the same time, unconditionally respect the gifts of the other people and understand how each contributes in reaching the objective.)

Judges 4-5 Deborah, a judge of Israel, is an administrator.

Neh. 1-7 Nehemiah demonstrates the qualities of an administrator.

Genesis 13; 14; 22-24 Abraham exhibits the traits of a giver.

Hosea 1:1-14:9 Hosea has the gift of prophecy.

Luke 2:36-38 The prophetic gift is demonstrated in Anna.

Luke 3:3-20; 7:18-29 The prophet gift is illustrated and John the Baptist is the example.

Luke 10:29-37 The good Samaritan shows the characteristics of the gift of mercy.

Luke 10:38-42; John 11:1-40; 12:2 Martha is portrayed as having the gift of server.

Acts 4:36; 11:23-26; 14:22; 15:2, 35-41 Barnabas' gift of exhortation is described.

Acts 9:36-42 The gift of giving is seen in Dorcas.

Acts 18:1-3, 24-28; Rom. 16: 3-5; 1 Cor. 16:19; 2 Tim. 4:19 Aquila and Priscilla demonstrate the gift of teaching.

Acts 18:24-28 Apollos is shown to have the gift of teaching.

Rom. 12:6-8 We have different gifts...let each use them in proportion.

Rom. 16:1-2 Phoebe's gift of serving is described.

1 Cor. 7:7 Each man has his own gift(s).

1 Cor. 12:1-12 There are different gifts but one Spirit.

1 Tim. 4:14-15 Do not neglect your gift; use it diligently.

1 Pet. 4:10-11 Each should use whatever gift he is given to serve others.

Anger/Temper

Prov. 15:1 A soft answer turns away wrath, but a harsh word stirs up anger. (RSV)

Prov. 15:18 A hot tempered man stirs up strife, but he who is slow to anger quiets contention. (RSV)

Prov. 16:32 Better a patient man than a warrior, a man who controls his temper than one who takes a city.

Prov. 19:19 A hot tempered man must pay the penalty; if you rescue him, you will have to do it again. (NIV)

Prov. 20:3 There is honor in avoiding strife.

Prov. 22:24-25 Do not associate with one easily angered.

Prov. 29:11 A fool gives full vent to his anger.

Prov. 29:22 An angry man stirs up dissension.

Eccl. 7:9 Do not be quickly provoked in your spirit.

Micah 7:18 You do not stay angry forever.

Eph. 4:31 Get rid of all anger.

Teaching (as teacher)

Prov. 13:1 A wise man heeds his father's instruction... (NIV)

Prov. 13:14 The teaching of the wise is a fountain of life, that one may avoid the snares of death. (RSV)

Mat. 13:51 Jesus asks if his students understand.

Col. 3:16 Let the word of Christ dwell in you richly, teach and admonish one another in all wisdom... (RSV)

2 Tim. 2:25 Those who oppose him he must gently instruct, in the hope that God will grant them repentance leading them to a knowledge of the truth. (NIV)

2 Tim. 3:16-17 Scripture is useful for teaching.

Wisdom

Prov. 3:13-14 Blessed is the man who finds wisdom.

Prov. 10:13 Wisdom is found on the lips of the discerning... (NIV)

Prov. 10:14 Wise men store up knowledge... (NIV)

Prov. 15:33 The fear of the Lord teaches a man wisdom, and humility comes before honor. (NIV)

Eccl. 1:18 For with much wisdom comes much sorrow; the more knowledge, the more grief. (NIV)

Isa. 5:13 Therefore my people will go into exile for lack of understanding. (NIV)

Advice (from God)

Deut. 8:3 God gave manna to teach that man does not live on bread alone but by His commandments.

1 Kings 22:5 ...First seek the counsel of the Lord... (NIV)

Psalm 16:7 I will praise the Lord who counsels me; even at night my heart instructs me. (NIV)

Psalm 32:8 I will instruct you and teach you the way you should go; I will counsel you with my eye upon you. (RSV)

Psalm 48:14 Our God will be our guide.

Prov. 2:6 The Lord gives wisdom and knowledge.

Prov. 16:20 Whoever gives heed to God's instruction prospers.

Isa. 48:17 I am the Lord your God who teaches you to profit, who leads you in the way you should go. (RSV)

Mat. 4:4 When Jesus was tempted by Satan, He responded that man does not live by bread alone but by every word that comes from the mouth of God.

Luke 4:4 Man does not live on bread alone.

John 10:27 My sheep hear my voice, and I know them, and they follow me... (RSV)

John 14:26 The Holy Spirit will teach you all things.

Advice (from others)

Job 21:16 ...so I stand aloof from the counsel of the wicked. (NIV)

Psalm 1:1 Blessed is the man who does not walk in the counsel of the wicked... (NIV)

Prov. 12:15 A wise man listens to advice.

Prov. 13:10 Wisdom is found in those who take advice.

Prov. 15:12 A mocker resents correction; he will not consult the wise. (NIV)

Prov. 15:22 Plans fail for lack of advice.

Prov. 19:20 Listen to advice and accept instruction, that you may gain wisdom for the future. (RSV)

Prov. 19:27 Stop listening to instruction and you will stray.

Prov. 20:18 Make plans by seeking advice.

Prov. 23:12 Apply your heart to instruction.

Prov. 27:17 As iron sharpens iron so one man sharpens another. (NIV)

Eccl. 7:5 It is better to heed a wise man's rebuke than to listen to the song of fools. (NIV)

Heb. 13:7-9 Do not be carried away by all kinds of strange teachings.

Communication

Gen. 11:1-9 A common language helped the Tower of Babel builders.

Prov. 15:4 The tongue that brings healing is a tree of life, but a deceitful tongue crushes the spirit. (NIV)

Prov. 22:21 Teaching you true and reliable words, so that you can give sound answers to him who sent you. (NIV)

Mat. 13:51 Jesus checked the audience to make sure they understood what he said.

V. MANAGEMENT: CONCEPTS AND SKILLS

Planning

Jer. 29:11-14 God has a plan for you.

Psalm 1:6 The Lord knows the way of the righteous.

Prov. 14:15 A simple man believes anything, but a prudent man gives thoughts to his steps. (NIV)

Prov. 15:22 Planning requires advice.

Prov. 16:3 Commit to the Lord whatever you do and your plans will be established. (RSV)

Prov. 16:9 A man's mind plans his way, but the Lord directs his steps. (RSV)

Prov. 19:21 Regardless of the man's plan, it is the Lord's purpose which will prevail, therefore seek the Lord's plan first.

Prov. 20:18 Seek advice when planning.

Prov. 20:24 A man's steps are directed by the Lord. How then can anyone understand his own way? (NIV)

Prov. 21:5 The plans of the diligent lead to profit as surely as haste leads to poverty. (NIV)

Prov. 29:18 Where there is no vision, the people perish: but he that keepeth the law, happy is he. (KJV)

Eccl. 9:11 Time and chance is involved.

Mat. 25:1-12 The parable of the ten maidens and the lamp oil is revealed. (Plan for needed supplies.)

Luke 12:30-31 Seek the Father first.

Luke 14:28-32 Plan the cost of a project before you start.

John 4:34 "My food...is to do the will of Him who sent me and to finish His work." (NIV) (The primary need is to do God's will.)

Strategy

Prov. 4:25-27 Let your eyes look straight ahead, fix your eyes directly before you. Make level paths for your feet and take only ways that are firm. Do not swerve to the right or the left; keep your foot from evil. (NIV)

Prov. 16:3 Commit your work to the Lord, and your plans will be established. (RSV)

Prov. 16:9 A man's mind plans his way, but the Lord directs his steps. (RSV)

Prov. 28:10 He who misleads the upright into an evil way will fall into his own pit... (RSV)

Eccl. 3:1-8 There is a time for everything.

Eccl. 8:6 There is a proper time and procedure for everything.

Lam. 3:40 Examine and test your plans.

Mat. 7:24 A wise builder knows the plans before he builds.

Mark 16:15 The goal was given but the strategy was left to the people who had been assigned the task.

Luke 6:47-49 Building a foundation.

Luke 16:8-9 Act shrewdly.

1 Thess. 5:24 When God calls you He will bring it to pass.

Knowing God's Will

Psalm 25:14 He who fears the Lord will be instructed by Him.

Prov. 19:21 The Lord's purpose will prevail.

Prov. 21:30 Nothing will succeed against the Lord.

Jer. 29:11-13 The Lord knows the plans He has for you.

Eph. 5:17 Don't be foolish, know what God's will is.

Zeph. 2:3 Seek the Lord.

Acts 4:28 The Lord decided beforehand what would happen.

Acts 5:38-39 If the plan is from God, you will not stop it.

God's Authority

Prov. 3:5-6 Trust in the Lord and not in yourself.

Phil. 2:13 For it is God who works in you, to will and to act for His good purpose. (NIV)

Knowledge

Psalm 32:8 God will instruct and counsel us.

Psalm 111:10 The fear of the Lord is the beginning of wisdom; a good understanding have all they that do his commandments; his praise endureth forever. (KJV)

Prov. 4:13 Hold on to instruction, do not let it go: guard it well, for it is your life. (NIV)

Prov. 8:10-12 Choose my instruction instead of silver, knowledge rather than choice gold, for wisdom is more precious than rubies and nothing you desire can compare with her. (NIV)

Prov. 12:23 A prudent man keeps his knowledge to himself, but the hearts of fools blurt out folly. (NIV)

Prov. 14:6 The mocker seeks wisdom and finds none, but knowledge comes easily to the discerning. (NIV)

Prov. 24:5 A wise man has great power, and a man of knowledge increases strength. (NIV)

Hosea 4:6 Destruction comes because of lack of knowledge.

Neh. 2:13-16 Nehemiah inspects the walls before rebuilding.

Mat. 7:7-12 Ask, seek and knock.

Budgeting

Prov. 22:3 Prudence looks for possible danger.

Luke 14:28-32 Estimate the costs.

Organizing

Span of Control

Exodus 18:21 Officers over thousands, hundreds, fifties, and tens.

1 Chr. 13:1 Commanders of thousands and hundreds.

2 Chr. 2:2 Solomon assigned seventy thousand men to bear burdens and eighty thousand to quarry in the hill country, and three thousand six hundred to oversee them. (RSV)

Unity

Gen. 11:6 If as one people...nothing...will be impossible. (NIV)

Psalm 133:1 How good it is when brothers live in unity. (NIV)

Amos 3:3 Do two walk together unless they have agreed to? (NIV)

Mat. 12:25; Mark 3:24-25; Luke 11:17 A kingdom divided against itself will not stand.

Acts 4:32 All the believers were one in heart and mind. (NIV)

1 Cor. 1:10 I appeal to you, brethren, by the name of our Lord Jesus Christ, that all of you agree and that there be no dissensions among you, but that you be united in the same mind and the same judgment. (RSV)

Phil. 2:2 Be like-minded.

Eph. 4:3 Then make my joy complete by being like minded, having the same love, being one in spirit and purpose. (NIV).

James 1:6 But let him ask in faith, with no doubting, for he who doubts is like a wave of the sea that is driven and tossed by the wind. (RSV)

1 Pet. 3:8 Finally, all of you, live in harmony with one another; be sympathetic, love as brothers, be compassionate and humble. (NIV)

Committees/Teams

Eccl. 4:9-12 Two are better than one...there is better return for the labor of a group. There is strength in numbers.

Mark 6:7-13 Jesus sends the disciples out in teams of two.

1 Cor. 12:14-26 All parts are necessary to function.

Overseers/Managers

1 Tim. 3:2-7; Tit. 1:7-9 Paul describes the characteristics of an overseer.

2 Tim. 2:24 Do not be quarrelsome.

Prov. 19:12 A king's wrath is like the growling of a lion, but his favor is like dew upon the grass. (RSV)

Division of Labor

Acts 6:1-4 Deacon positions were created to care for widows.

Eph. 4:11-12 Some are to be apostles, prophets, evangelists, etc.

Staffing

Arbitration

Job 31:13-14 If...denied justice to servants... what will God do to me? (NIV)

Mat. 18:15-17 Talk to your brother, then with a witness, then go to the church (to a higher authority in the organization) with your concerns.

Selection

Ex. 18:21 Select capable men who fear God.

Mat. 4:18-22; Mark 3:13-15; Luke 6:12-16 Jesus selected the disciples.

John 15:16 Jesus has chosen and appointed us.

1 Tim. 3:2-7; Tit. 1:7-9 Paul describes the characteristics of an overseer.

2 Tim. 2:24 Do not be quarrelsome.

Interviewing

Prov. 20:5 Draw out the purpose of a man's heart.

Gifts

Rom. 12:6-8 We have different gifts...let each use them in proportion. (NIV)

1 Cor. 7:7 Each man has his own gift(s).

1 Cor. 12:1-12 There are different gifts but one Spirit.

1 Tim. 4:14-15 Do not neglect your gift; use it diligently.

1 Pet. 4:10 ...each should use whatever gift he has been given to serve others. (NIV)

Discipline

Prov. 6:23 ...the corrections of discipline are a way of life. (NIV)

Prov. 12:1 He who loves discipline loves knowledge. (RSV)

Prov. 13:18 He who ignores discipline comes to poverty and shame. (NIV)

Prov. 13:24 He who spares the rod hates his son, he who loves him is careful to discipline him. (NIV)

Prov. 15:5 ...but whoever heeds correction shows prudence. (NIV)

Prov. 15:10 ...he who hates correction will die. (NIV)

Prov. 15:32 ...whoever heeds correction gains understanding. (NIV)

Prov. 17:10 A rebuke goes deeper into a man of understanding than a hundred blows into a fool. (RSV)

Prov. 19:18 Discipline your son while there is hope; do not set your heart on his destruction. (RSV)

Prov. 19:25 ...rebuke a discerning man and he will gain knowledge. (NIV)

Prov. 25:12 Like a gold ring or an ornament of gold is a wise reprover to a listening ear. (RSV)

Prov. 29:1 A man who remains stiff-necked after many rebukes will suddenly be destroyed—without remedy. (NIV)

Prov. 29:15 The rod of correction imparts wisdom... (NIV)

Heb. 12:11 For the moment all discipline seems painful rather than pleasant; later it yields the peaceful fruit of righteousness to those who have been trained by it. (RSV)

Teaching

Prov. 6:23 For the commandment is a lamp and the teaching a light... (RSV)

Prov. 11:14 For lack of guidance a nation falls... (NIV)

Prov. 13:13 He who scorns instruction will pay for it, but he who respects a command is rewarded. (NIV)

Prov. 16:20 Whoever gives heed to instruction prospers. (NIV)

Prov. 16:23 A wise man's heart guides his mouth, and his lips promote instruction. (NIV)

Prov. 22:6 Train up a child in the way he should go, and when he is old he will not depart from it. (RSV)

Luke 6:40 A student is not above his teacher, but everyone who is fully trained will be like his teacher. (NIV)

James 3:1 Let not many of you become teachers, my brethren, for you know that we who teach shall be judged with greater strictness. (RSV)

Knowledge of Employees

Prov. 27:23 Know well the condition of your flocks, and give attention to your herds... (RSV) As flocks were entrusted for safe keeping to the stewardship of shepherds, so are employees entrusted to the stewardship of managers.

Evaluating

Mat. 7:3-5; Luke 6:41-42 Why…look for a speck when there is a plank in your own eye.

John 7:24 Do not judge by appearances, but judge with right judgment. (RSV) When evaluating employees, make your judgment on the facts, not on an inappropriate base.

James 3:9-12 With the tongue we praise our Lord and Father, and with it we curse men, who have been made in God's likeness. Out of the same mouth come praise and cursing, My brothers, this should not be. Can both fresh water and salt water flow from the same spring? My brothers, can a fig tree bear olives, or a grapevine bear figs? Neither can a salt spring produce fresh water. (NIV) (The comparison of salt water and fresh water has parallels to the heart of the manager and how he talks about employees. If his heart is directed towards God, how can he speak poorly about employees?)

Authority over Employees

Col. 3:22-25 Slaves (employees) obey your earthly masters (supervisors).

Col. 4:1 Masters, provide your slaves with what is right and fair, for you know that you also have a Master in heaven. (NIV)

Recognition of employees

Prov. 3:27 Do not withhold good from those who deserve it, when it is within your power to act. (NIV)

Mat. 25:21 The master recognized good works.

Phil. 2:4 Look to the interests of others.

Directing
Standards
Isa. 5:10 A ten acre vineyard will produce a bath of wine.

Production of goods
Mat. 3:10; Luke 3:9 A tree that doesn't produce good fruit will be cut down.

Luke 13:6-9 A non-producing fig tree is cut down.

John 15:4 A branch can't bear fruit alone; it needs the vine.

Decisions
Num. 13:17-20 Moses sent spies to investigate.

Prov. 16:33 The lot is cast into the lap, but the decision is wholly from the Lord. (RSV)

Prov. 18:13 Hear everything before answering.

Prov. 19:2 Study the facts.

Luke 14:31-32 Consider the alternatives.

VI. LEADERSHIP CHARACTERISTICS

1 Sam. 13:14 The Lord has sought out a man after his own heart.

1 Sam. 9:16 I will send you a man...anoint him leader over my people.

2 Sam. 23:3-4 When a just man rules in the fear of God, he is like the light of morning at sunrise.

Prov. 6:16-19 There are six things the Lord hates, seven that are detestable to him: haughty eyes, a lying tongue, hands that shed innocent blood, a heart that devises wicked schemes, feet that are quick to rush into evil, a false witness who pours out lies and a man who stirs up dissensions among brothers. (NIV)

Prov. 28:2-3 A man of understanding and knowledge maintains order.

Isa. 33:15-16 Isaiah describes a leader as one who walks righteously, speaks what is right, rejects gain from extortion, keeps his hand from accepting bribes, stops his ears against plots of murder, and shuts his eyes against contemplating evil.

Isa. 55:4 I have made him a witness to the people...a leader and commander for the people. (RSV)

Acts 20:28 Keep watch over yourselves and all the flock of which the Holy Spirit has made you overseers. (NIV)

1 Tim. 3:1-12 Paul describes the characteristics of an overseer.

Titus 1:7 ...overseer...must be blameless—not overbearing, not quick tempered, not given to drunkenness, not violent, not pursuing dishonest gain.

1 Peter 5:2-4 ...overseers...as God wants you to be; not greedy for money, but eager to serve; not lording it over those entrusted to you, but being examples to the flock.

Entrepreneurship

Acts 18:2,3 Paul stays with Aquila and Priscilla who were tentmakers like himself.

APPENDIX A: MANAGING BY BEATITUDES

Management is a collection of activities by which we accomplish tasks, objectives and goals to fulfill the mission of our organizations. There are many definitions of management. You may not agree with all of them and I understand if you do not completely agree with me. I hope, first, that you do agree with me that managers must affect others to accomplish anything; and second, that who we are and how we behave have greater impact on the people managed than what we say.

This document is written from the perspective that Christ is the Messiah, the living God and that the Bible is God's truth written through inspired authors. My premise is that the Bible is a life-plan, or an "owner's manual" for us. The Bible affects managers as much as any other vocation. Managers, for too long, left the Bible to Sunday morning and allowed it to gather dust during the week. Many managers even read the Bible daily to see how it should affect their lives, yet never make the connection to their managerial activities and life. Since most managers work more than 50 hours a week, it seems that there is a significant amount of a manager's life that is "Bible-less."

I wrote this document to show the manager how the Word of God gives attitude and behavior parameters for that important 50+ hours a week that they are in contact with, and managing through, people.

The Sermon on the Mount, as recorded in the Gospel according to Matthew, is a powerful message from Jesus on lifestyle and behavior. Augustine referred to it as the highest standard of morality and as the perfect measure of the Christian life (Kissinger, 1975, p. 13).

Thomas Aquinas considered the messages from the Sermon on the Mount as wise counsel. Aquinas went on to differentiate these counsels from commandments. Aquinas described commandments as obligations whereas counsels were left to the option of each person who hears them (Kissinger, 1975, p. 13). Most commentaries I read refer to the Sermon on the Mount as the basis for ethical behavior.

The Beatitudes comprise the ten verses from Matthew 5:3-12. These ten verses contain eight statements of counsel. Popular translations of the Bible separate the Beatitudes into verses. The original Greek, however, shows them as one continuous flowing thought. This is important for today's manager because the message of the Beatitudes must be taken in the whole and not as an *a la carte* menu. The people whom we manage see our attitudes, ethics and beliefs in total.

Each statement of counsel begins with the Greek word *makarios,* which translated into English is "blessed." *Makarios is* akin to the Hebrew Word "shalom." Augsburger describes the word as "incorporating the meaning of wholeness, of joy, of well-being, of holistic peace..., of the condition of inner satisfaction expressed by Jesus in John 14:27 'My peace I give unto you: not as the world giveth'" (KJV) (Augsburger, 1982, p. 63).

The original Greek leaves out the verb form of "to be," thus removing the sense of time. These words of counsel are intended to be timeless, neither to be in the future, past, nor present, but in all time and throughout all time.

When you read the Beatitudes below, read them as one thought, inseparable, with the view of timeless application.

Matthew 5:3-12

> 3 Blessed are the poor in spirit, for theirs is the kingdom of heaven.
>
> 4 Blessed are those who mourn, for they will be comforted.
>
> 5 Blessed are the meek, for they will inherit the earth.
>
> 6 Blessed are those who hunger and thirst for righteousness, for they will be filled.
>
> 7 Blessed are the merciful, for they will be shown mercy.

8 Blessed are the pure in heart, for they will see God.

9 Blessed are the peacemakers, for they will be called sons of God.

10 Blessed are those who are persecuted because of righteousness, for theirs is the kingdom of heaven.

11 Blessed are you when people insult you, persecute you and falsely say all kinds of evil against you because of me.

12 Rejoice and be glad, because great is your reward in heaven, for in the same way they persecuted the prophets who were before you.

Blessed are the poor in spirit, for theirs is the kingdom of heaven

"Poor in spirit" is a state opposite of "rich in pride." What a paradox! Managers always look up to the "king of the hill" who is full of bravado and proud of his accomplishments. This Beatitude says to avoid that pride and see yourself as being empty. An empty cup can hold much, but a full cup can receive nothing more. A full cup must live on what it already contains, nothing more.

The Greek words better translate to "Blessed are you poor," (Baker, 1963, p. 30) which connotes someone who knows he is poor. This is an excellent definition for one who is humble. Scripture is replete with references to the need to be, and remain, humble. Isaiah 26:5 talks of God humbling those who dwell on high; Matthew 18:4 and 23:12 speak of the need to be humble. Isaiah 66:2 refers to the man who is humble and contrite in spirit. Spirit in the Isaiah passage is the Hebrew word *ruwach* which translates as "the spirit of a rational being." The Greek word used in Matthew 5:3 is *pneuma,* translated as "human spirit" or "rational soul."

The first Beatitude counsels the manager to be humble, not haughty. This ties into the scriptural admonition to not lord it over our employees (Matthew 20:24-28). Consider the positive characteristic of the manager to be humble and contrite of spirit with regard to his employees. The manager who is poor of spirit knows that his employees are intelligent people who, many times, know more of the details of the job-tasks performed and, thus, have worthwhile advice to give. This is a key premise of total quality management—to teach the employees how to solve problems, develop solutions, and then trust them to do the work. A humble manager does not lord it over his employees and force answers and solutions upon them.

A humble manager is teachable. The cocky know-it-all manager is so full of himself that there is no room for God's kingdom in his daily life. God looks for the humble to fill them with His kingdom. Can you think of managers who

mentored potential up-and-coming junior managers? Only the poor in spirit can be taught.
Why should God spend time training the un-
trainable? The same is true for managers men-
toring employees.

A humble manager shows respect to all, whether
to superiors or subordinates. This concept of
respect is important to consider. Would you
rather work for someone who treats you with
respect or treats you as dirt to be walked upon?
The answer is obvious. We all look forward to
working with manager/bosses who are kind,
considerate and look upon us as co-workers
rather than slaves to abuse.

Humbleness of spirit is important in reaching the
mission of the organization. A humble manager
places the goals of the organization above his
own goals. The haughty manager looks for how
the organization can help him achieve his own
goals.

This humbleness does not mean poor in finances
or ability. I know a wonderful man who, some
time ago, retired from an international bank as
senior vice-president (the number two spot in a
multinational firm). He was certainly wealthy in
terms of cash—he received lavish compensation
during his career and invested excess earnings
into a sizable fortune. He owned homes in both
Seattle and Palm Springs and enjoyed playing
golf in many places around the world. The first

characteristic you recognized in this man was his humility. He listened to those who talked and placed the needs of others before his own. His employees maintained incredibly loyalty to him and spent many extra hours accomplishing the work of the organization because they delighted in serving <u>with</u> him rather than being mere tools to use and discard.

The essence of excellent customer service is the subjugation of our own interests, feelings and self-aggrandizement to the needs, wants and desires of our clients. Blanchard, in his book <u>Raving Fans</u> consistently shows that the manager who creates "raving fans" places his interest behind the interest of the client.

Sometimes it feels like you are losing when you yield to another. The paradox of Jesus' teaching is that, although you feel like you are losing, you are winning. My banking friend was humble and consistently rose to the top. Blanchard's case studies describe people whose companies do well and improve daily. Clients flock to companies that delight them. Employees gravitate to humble managers who treat them well.

Humbleness does not mean avoiding the limelight. A great actor goes on stage to serve his customers and delight his audience. His entire being is placed into the performance. If he does his best, he is satisfied. If the audience is satisfied enough to applaud, so much the better. If a standing ovation is given, he accepts it warmly and appreciatively and the next morning continues with rehearsal to ensure that he delights the next client. The applause is icing on the cake and is akin to the saying "money follows ministry." If the actor sets out only to gain a standing ovation, he serves himself rather than others.

Success is doubtful in this situation. Thus we face the paradox again. Try not to achieve, but to serve and delight, and success will follow; try to succeed for selfish gain and fail.

How much more could a humble manager accomplish with eight employees working hard to please him, compared to a haughty manager with eight employees who care less if the manager lived or died? Blessed is the manager who is poor in spirit, for his shall be the kingdom of heaven.

Blessed are those who mourn, for they will be comforted

The paradox of each of these counsels is dramatic. Here we receive instruction to mourn because we will be comforted. The world prefers to cast off mourners and shun those who grieve. The world seeks out those who are happy and excited. We smile at the jokes of the salesman and gather at the table of the motivational speaker to be fired up and pumped with enthusiasm. Why then would we want to become mourners?

The Greek word we translate "to mourn" is the strongest of the Greek words which implore a deep mourning and longing. The word is also used to mourn for the dead (Augsburger, 1982, p. 63). We are interested in the living manager—not the dead. Consider this word to show the intensity at which we mourn for those around us. To mourn in this fashion is to care deeply, to care for the organization, to care for the clients that we serve, to care for our employees, to care for our superiors, and to care for the condition of our competitors. This is not exhaustive of the list, but rather a means of beginning. To mourn this deeply is to draw closer to God and for God to draw closer to you (Augsburger, 1982, p. 63).

The Greek word we translate here as "mourn" is *penteo* which is the act or feeling of mourning or bewailing. This is an active tense verb which implies a continuation of action. Think of the manager who cares so much about his employees, his clients, his company, his market, his superiors and his competitors that he literally is in mourning for their condition. This state of mourning is characterized by a deep concern. It does not imply that the manager goes around the office crying, yelling, beating his chest and pulling out his hair. It does imply that there is great concern for others.

Have you ever worked for someone who cared about you—really cared? Loyalty and devotion to task and company grow out of trust and a knowledge of protection which comes from the employment relationship. Employees who know the manager has their interests at heart will commit themselves to the corporate tasks. This is the same condition that Scripture says must be created between husband and wife. The husband must care so much for his wife that his every decision is filtered through the question, "is it in the best interest of my wife?"

Consider what it would be like to work for a manager who was so concerned about you that he treated you as a co-worker (from the first Beatitude), and cared so deeply about you that he made decisions with your interests in mind. This is certainly not the typical United States manager. The paradox of Scripture implies the same as the great admonition of Jesus that whoever is to be first must be last. Great managers do not seek to be number one; they become number one because their employees make them number one. Innovation in a company is always at the discretion of the employees. Just as you can lead a horse to water and not be able to make it drink, so also you can lead an employee to the edge of innovation and excellence, but you cannot make him jump the line to improvement. He will only do that because he wants to.

William Arnold's book <u>The Human Touch</u> gives us an inside look at a CEO who cared for and mourned for his employees. The employees of the Hospital Corporation of America consistently sought ways of improving the organization from the vice-president of finance to the janitors and the valet car parking attendants.

Blessed are those managers who mourn for their employees and their customers, for they will be comforted and see improvement.

Blessed are the meek, for they will inherit the earth

Today's typical manager abhors the word "meek." Managers want employees to know that they are the boss. The popular management press is awash with books on tough negotiation styles, and the business magazines write about the toughest bosses in the toughest companies. Jesus' counsel again shows the depth of the paradox in the characteristics that he seeks in us.

The Greek word for meek is *praus,* or humility, which continues the theme of humility from the first Beatitude. This is not a repetition of the first Beatitude, for what would be the purpose of repeating a characteristic? Rather it is an application of humility to behavior. *Praus* is also found in conjunction with action. It is thought of in connection with discipline. The meek have a sense of duty and demon-strate controlled discipline. Aristotle spoke of meekness as the means between anger and indifference (Augsburger, 1982, p. 63). Aristotle described one who is meek as being angry on the right occasion with the right people at the right moment and for the right length of time (Boice, 1972, p. 37).

Barclay stated that selfish anger is always a sin but selfless anger can be one of the great moral dynamics of the world (Barclay, 1958, p. 91). We see this controlled selfless anger in Jesus as he swept the money changers out of the temple. (Matthew 21:12-13). The psalmist wrote of the meek inheriting the earth (Psalm 37:11). The Hebrew word used by the psalmist here is *anayv* which translates to "gentle in mind or circumstances." It is also used to denote saintliness.

A biblical example of a meek man is Moses. "Now the man Moses was very meek, above all the men who were upon the face of the earth" (Numbers 12:3). The Hebrew word for meek here is the same that the psalmist used. Note that Moses is described as being above all the men who were upon the face of the earth. Not your idea of a mild-mannered little man with limited strength and force-of-will. Moses defeated the gods of Egypt, conquered the pharaoh, led a million people out of bondage, fed and cared for them for over 40 years, laid down the Mosaic Law, and established the foundation for the promised land of Israel. Moses did not do this alone; God worked through Moses to accomplish all these feats. God can only work through the humbleness, the mourning and the disciplined anger of those managers who, as empty vessels, can be filled by Him.

Charles Wesley's hymn is used by Baker to demonstrate the strength and controlled discipline:

Jesus' tremendous name
   Puts all our foes to flight:
Jesus, the meek, the angry Lamb
   A Lion is in fight.
   By all hell's host withstood,
   We all hell's host o'erthrow:
And conquering them, through Jesus' blood,
   We still to conquer go. (Baker, 1963, p.
   44)

Baker continues his definition of meek by saying "the meek man never submits to evil or compromises with it, but by active, persistent patience overcomes it" (Baker, 1963, p. 45). Bauman gives us another view of meek. Bauman describes the characteristic of meek as a "wild animal who, upon domestication, is still just as capable of feats of strength, yet gentle with people." Bauman repeats his definition as "power under control" (Bauman, 1981, p. 56).

Consider the manager who possesses controlled discipline. He never flies off the handle, yells, or shouts at those who work for him. He remains in control of his faculties at all times. He holds to his values and never compromises them in order to get the next promotion or to get the next big order. He is seen by those around him as a rock of strength and controlled energy, unflappable in the midst of confusion and frustration. The meek manager is seen as someone whom you can confide in because he never strikes back if he hears criticism.

> *Great men suffer hours of depression through introspection and self-doubt. That is why they are great. That is why you will find modesty and humility the characteristics of such men.—Bruce Barton*

Imagine working for a manager like this. Would you give your all for this manager? Would you go the extra mile without being asked? Most employees would. Blessed are the meek managers, for their controlled discipline will result in inheriting the earth.

Blessed are those who hunger and thirst for righteousness, for they will be filled

This Beatitude speaks of the attitude of the manager toward a right-relationship with God. The words "hunger" and "thirst" in the Greek are *peinao* and *dipsao* meaning, respectively, "famished" or "crave for," and "to thirst for." These words imply an ongoing condition. This is similar to the condition described in Psalm 42:1,2a "As the deer pants for streams of water, so my soul pants for you, O God. My soul thirsts for God, for the living God" (NIV). We translate "righteousness" from the Greek word *dikaisoune* which comes from the Greek word *dikaios*. This root word *dikaios* and its derivative *dikaisoune* can be translated as "holy, just, right(eous), equity (of character or act)." We begin to see the unfolding of an ethical man. Eric Baker described the person in this way: "the man who is blessed in this respect is the man who above all desires to fulfill the intention of his being and become what he ought to be" (Baker, 1963, p. 55).

This Beatitude is often presumed to mean the seeking after God only. Jesus placed this Beatitude in the fourth position. It follows the thought pattern of asking people to be humble, to be mournful of the problems and conditions around us, to be controlled in our actions, and now He is asking the manager to continually seek what is good, what is just, what is right, and what is equitable. Imagine the manager who holds these four characteristics.

We have only traveled through the first half of the Beatitudes and already the Beatitudes build a manager with more interest in people and his organization, with more concern and more righteousness than 90% of the typical managers in

American organizations today (my presumption).

Jesus builds a perfect manager by starting with a key foundation stone and adding character blocks. Each block appears intriguing by itself, but combined with the others creates a building. Watch for the future blocks Jesus adds to the perfect manager.

Each of us know desires that we hunger and thirst after. Jesus used these verbs for a reason. Hunger and thirst are primary activities. Some would say instinctual—activities that always take place. Yet, we also hunger and thirst after the unrighteous, the unjust, the inequitable, the unholy. Jesus recognizes the free-will of man and differentiates the manager who seeks what is good from the one who seeks what is not good. Blessed is he who seeks good. There is an unstated thought that the one who seeks what is not good will not be blessed. Notice there is not a condemnation in this passage, only a support for right behavior.

Consider what it might be like to work for a manager who always seeks what is right, just, equitable, and holy. The manager constantly looks for opportunities to do good deeds for the organization. The manager constantly watches himself, ensuring that he keeps his own mind and body free of unhealthy actions. This manager certainly would not be one whom we would expect to see before a grand jury for embezzlement or in a hospital suffering from a coronary at age 45! This manager could even run for national political office with a clear conscience that even the most "dogged" reporter could not turn up any dirt to shame his character.

I am not describing a "holier-than-thou," self-righteous, Bible-thumping workplace berater of what everyone else should do. Remember the first three Beatitudes. The perfect manager is first humble. That means that while he is seeking righteousness, he does it because he just knows it is right. He may not be aware that he is doing the "right" thing, he just does it. He is the manager whom others talk about with quiet respect and admiration wishing they could be as good and wondering how he does it. It is interesting to point out that if others wish to learn how to be like this perfect manager they could learn by reading a single text—the Bible!

You will know the righteous manager by the evidence of the presence of the Holy Spirit. Isaiah 11:1-5 provides a description of the presence of the Holy Spirit. This passage describes the coming Messiah. The righteous manager will also manifest these same characteristics.

> *A shoot will come up from the stump of Jesse;*
> *   from his roots a Branch will bear fruit.*
> *The Spirit of the LORD will rest on him—*

> *the Spirit of wisdom and of*
> *understanding,*
> *the Spirit of counsel and of power,*
> *the Spirit of knowledge and of the fear*
> *of the LORD—*
> *and he will delight in the fear of the LORD.*
>
> *He will not judge by what he sees with his*
> *eyes,*
>> *or decide by what he hears with his*
>> *ears;*
> *but with righteousness he will judge the*
> *needy,*
>> *with justice he will give decisions for the*
>> *poor of the earth.*
> *He will strike the earth with the rod of his*
> *mouth;*
>> *with the breath of his lips he will slay*
>> *the wicked.*
> *Righteousness will be his belt*
>> *and faithfulness the sash around his*
>> *waist.*

The manager who seeks righteousness will be filled with it. You will know he is filled by the presence of the Spirit of wisdom and understanding, of counsel and of power, and having a knowledge of God and a fear of God.

Wisdom and understanding go together. The Hebrew for wisdom here is *chokmah* which is derived from the root *chakam* meaning "to be wise in mind, act and word; to deal wisely, to

88

make wiser." The action tense "to make" is the key. The manager's actions tell us if wisdom is present. The Hebrew word we translate as "understanding" is *biynah* which is derived from *biyn* which is freely translated "to separate mentally." It can also be translated as "perceive, to be prudent, to teach, think or cause to make happen." Wisdom means knowing what is right for the situation and understanding means the ability to put action to the thoughts. Hence the righteous manager not only knows what is correct, but implements plans to bring about correct action.

Counsel and power are placed together in this passage to build on each other and to grow from the foundation of wisdom and understanding. *Etsah,* the Hebrew word for counsel means "advice" or "prudence." It is a word which closely aligns with *ya'ats* meaning "to give and take advice, to determine, to purpose, and to guide." Power is sometimes translated as might (King James Version); both power and might translate from the Hebrew *gebuwrah* which means "valor, victory, force, mastery, power, strength, and might." This word picture shows us the righteous manager as one who not only knows what is right and devises action steps to bring about correct action, but also seeks advice and advises people around him as to what to do. In addition, he possesses the power, strength, or resources to enact the right action.

The Hebrew for knowledge implies a knowledge of Jehovah. The righteous manager knows God and fears Him. This fear is not a fear of cowering and concern for life and limb. This fear is of respect and acceptance of the "awesomeness" that is God. Have you ever worked for a manager that was so good, so powerful, so knowledgeable, so capable that you could not help being in awe and amazed? Those who have worked with righteous managers tell me they are in fear of the greatness of the man, yet the manager does nothing to cause them to be afraid (as in a fear for safety). This completion of the word picture lets us see that the righteous manager does all things in the knowledge of God and with a deep respect for the person of God manifested as the Holy Spirit.

> *Fear [the fear of man—not respect] is an acid which is pumped into one's atmosphere. It causes mental, moral and spiritual asphyxiation and sometimes death; death to energy and all growth.—Horace Fletcher*

The manager who seeks after what is good, righteous, just, holy and equitable does so in all phases of his life whether in the office, the home, the church or on the sports field. He seeks what is good for other departments in his company even if it means that his own department must give up something to improve the life of another. He understands the spiritual laws of Reciprocity, Unity, and Greatness (Robertson,

1992). He is the type of manager that other department heads seek for information and advice. He is the person who most often can speak at a meeting and bring quiet and peace to the table.

This condition of the ideal manager is not so difficult to attain as it might seem on the surface. Note the Beatitude says that if the manager truly seeks after that which is good, right, holy, just, and equitable, he will be filled. The use of the verb form "will be" is future-present tense meaning an activity which must follow another. If you truly seek what is good, you will be given it. Simple, isn't it?

Blessed are the merciful,
for they will be shown mercy

This Beatitude focuses on the Law of Reciprocity (Robertson, 1992). Be merciful and you will be shown mercy. The Greek word used here, *eleemon,* does translate equitably into English as "compassionate" or "merciful." There are two interesting aspects of this word. The first is that it is an active tense. The manager must be merciful in the current sense of the word. The second point of interest is that this word is only used one other time in the New Testament—Hebrew 2:17 which says: "...a merciful and faithful high priest in service to God and that he might make atonement for the sins of the people."

Shakespeare wrote that "...mercy seasons justice." This is the essence of this Beatitude to the manager. Mercy implies an understanding heart applied to the situation of judgment. Managers must make decisions and decide correctness from incorrectness with regard to employees' behavior.

Human justice is rough and blundering, full of rules and regulations. Little regard seems to exist for the person or the long-term learning which might come out of a situation. God showed a measure of mercy toward Sodom and Gomorra when Abraham pleaded for the cities. Mercy does not condone sin or wrongdoing in the workplace. Mercy commands that the manager first examine the heart of the employee. The manager must consider if the employee sees the action as wrong. If the employee confesses against the wrong action and shows repentance (a turning away from the action), then the manager must show mercy in his judgment.

Matthew 18:26-35 provides a parable of a young man who was forgiven and then dealt with harshly after he showed no mercy to those who owed him money. God forgives us our sins when we first come to Him and then again as we seek forgiveness and demonstrate repentance. I am grateful that He does, for many of my past actions deserved stiff punishment.

The parable of the prodigal son, found in Luke 15:11-31, offers an example of how a manager exhibits the Beatitude of showing mercy. The son deserved nothing from his father. The son already received and squandered his inheritance. Yet, his father knew of the good within his son and looked forward to the future times when they would accomplish much together. Mercy allows us to forgive and forget that which is not necessary for the future. Be careful here that you see true repentance in the prodigal son, a true understanding of the wrongfullness of his actions and a desire to see restitution and reunion with his father.

Contrast this with a situation involving an atheist manager. He offended a Christian employee and when the employee commented on her feelings, the atheist manager responded, "You're a Christian so you must forgive me as many times as I offend you. I've got it easy, you've got it hard, ha!" The atheist needs to realize that repentance goes before forgiveness and right action follows forgiveness. Mercy does not mean accepting another walking on or abusing you.

Imagine working for the merciful manager. You know if you do wrong that you expect the manager to call you on the carpet for clarification and redress. You know this and appreciate the teaching. Proverbs contains many references to the wise person seeking and accepting reproof. As you enter the manager's office, you know that you can expect to receive a measure of mercy and compassion. Your intentions were good even if your behavior was misguided. Later, when the manager makes a mistake and causes you difficulty, you willingly forgive and administer a measure of mercy to him as well. Do you think that you might defend the manager to other employees because he took your side with his superiors? Most employees desire to work for a merciful manager and are quite willing to give mercy in return.

> *O man, forgive thy mortal foe*
> *nor ever strike him blow for blow,*
> *For all the saints on earth that live*
> *To be forgiven must forgive,*
> *For all the blessed souls in heaven*
> *Are both forgivers and forgiven*
> *(Baker, 1963, p. 66).*

Blessed is the manager who shows compassion and mercy to the people who work with him, for his employees show him an equal amount of compassion and mercy.

Blessed are the pure in heart, for they will see God

The pure in heart speaks of integrity. The Greek *katharos* used in this Beatitude means to be clean, clear, or pure. This would be the same as undefiled, unblemished. The intent here is the same as the Greek *amiantos* referred to in 1 Pe-

ter 1:4 which translates "pure" or "undefiled."
The Greek word *kardia* from which we get heart
in this passage is also translated as the thoughts
or feelings (the mind). The manager should be
clean and undefiled in his thoughts and feelings.
This definition goes beyond the ability to act
"well", to "behave" or to "control our thoughts."
It is not acceptable to have unclean thoughts and
then suppress them. The concept of pure is that
there is no contamination at all. The Pharisees of
Jesus' time tried to act pure and cover up their
iniquities. Jesus exposed them for their true
thoughts and feelings.

This is a tough request for most managers. Not
only are managers called to be merciful, but they
are called to have only good thoughts and feelings about other people and attitudes. If we look
at this Beatitude only with respect to the manager dealing with peers, we conclude that the
workplace would be free of gossip and ill-will
between functional areas. We would tear down
the walls we have built and replace them with
arches (Winston, 1993).

This Beatitude speaks of focus. The definition of
pure can also be "unmixed." The manager is
called to be focused on the mission of the organization. The need for unity and pureness of
thought and feeling is critical to the support of
the next Beatitude. Notice how each Beatitude
builds on the others. Each one, seemingly, is

incomplete without the others to form a perfect picture of the perfect manager.

The justification for purity of heart is grand—to see God. This Beatitude leads me to believe that only the pure of heart, those with integrity, those with a focus on one God, will be able to see God. The manager can only see God if there is nothing between him and the Master. The manager may have other loyalties, but they must be subordinate to God. The manager must be single-minded and focused first on serving and loving God. Kierkegaard said that purity of heart is "to will one thing."

It is difficult to apply action steps to this condition of purity of heart. David was frustrated with the same desire to understand how to be pure in heart. He records his words in Psalm 51:6-12:

> *Surely you desire truth in the inner parts;*
> *you teach me wisdom in the inmost place.*
>
> *Cleanse me with hyssop, and I will be clean;*
> *wash me, and I will be whiter than snow.*
> *Let me hear joy and gladness;*
> *let the bones you have crushed rejoice.*
> *Hide your face from my sins*

> *and blot out all my iniquity.*
>
> *Create in me a pure heart, O God,*
> *and renew a steadfast spirit within*
> *me.*
> *Do not cast me from your presence*
> *or take your Holy Spirit from me.*
> *Restore to me the joy of your salvation*
> *and grant me a willing spirit, to*
> *sustain me. (NIV)*

The process of gaining a pure heart is to ask God for assistance. Managers are human with all the human frailties and faults. To be pure is difficult and cannot be achieved on our own. The help of the Holy Spirit is crucial to the manager becoming pure in heart, just as knowing God can only occur with His help.

Blessed are the peacemakers, for they will be called sons of God

This Beatitude goes beyond the concept of people waving white flags, or singing 'We are the World." This Beatitude has direct implication to the manager. The Greek word *eirenopoios* is used here for peacemaker. This word is derived from *eirene* meaning "one, peace, quietness, rest" and *poieo* meaning "to make or do." A manager must be one who causes peace, who causes quietness and rest. This is a far cry from the image most managers project. Imagine working for a manager who strives to maintain a sense of peace and rest in the workplace. This does not imply a slow, dull work environment. There is great speed in the movement of a hummingbird's wings and a fast motion to its flight, yet, when you watch the small bird, there appears to be a great peace about it. A similar physical sense can be felt if you go to a large aquarium. Many major cities maintain large aquariums with gigantic holding tanks. There the big fish swim with strength and speed, yet here too there seems to be a sense of peace and tranquility, a sense of harmony and unity.

The essence of this Beatitude is that the manager must seek to build and sustain unity in the workplace. Note I used the two verbs "build" and "sustain." In Genesis, the Hebrew word for create is *bara* and implies a formative condition—to create and sustain. By building and sustaining unity, the manager sets a condition in the workplace where conflict cannot gain a foothold. Just think of how much time and effort is wasted suffering from conflict or trying to resolve it. The court systems are backlogged with millions of cases seeking judicial resolution to conflict. We are a conflict-seeking people. How much more could we do if we channeled all the energy, effort, and resources spent, because of conflict, into feeding the hungry, healing the sick, and educating the children. Much of the problem in the African nations today would go away if the managers there remove the conditions for conflict (my presumption only).

Peacemakers are rare. To build and sustain unity, thus removing conflict, requires humility, wisdom, knowledge, mercy, and purity in heart. Does this sound familiar? Re-examine the last three Beatitudes and see the characteristics of each. To make and sustain peace is an exacting labor-intensive process. Peace does not occur because we do nothing. Peace is not an absence of strife. Peace must be maintained.

The manager must first make peace in his own life before he can successfully make peace in his organization. A manager in conflict with himself is a house divided. Jesus talked of a divided house in Matthew 12:25: Jesus knew their thoughts and said to them, "Every kingdom divided against itself will be ruined, and every city or household divided against itself will not stand." When there is spiritual unity in the heart of the manager, then, and only then, can he move out to create and sustain peace in the organization.

This Beatitude is the last Beatitude with a request to take action or display a characteristic. The other blessings have led up to this one. Look at the reward for this characteristic. The manager will be called a son of God. See how these last three Beatitudes have transitioned in their blessings. The manager will know God, he will see God and now he will be called a son of God. In the time of Jesus, the act of calling someone a son was to adopt the person and give the adoptee all inheritance rights.

Blessed are those who are persecuted because of righteousness, for theirs is the kingdom of heaven

Blessed are you when people insult you, persecute you and falsely say all kinds of evil against you because of me

Rejoice and be glad, because great is your reward in heaven, for in the same way they persecuted the prophets who were before you

These three, although stated as three verses, seem to represent one characteristic—suffering persecution. Thus, I combine them into the eighth characteristic.

Righteousness is the same word used in the fourth Beatitude—*dikaisoune*. This Beatitude is a call to commitment. A manager who commits to integrity and seeking that which is right(eous), holy, good, and equitable must stand for what he believes. To not stand for your commitment negates the value of the ethical statements.

Consider the manager who is asked to write a report recommending that his department undertake a new project. The manager has put forward a belief among those who work with him that he believes in what is righteous. The employees believe him and trust him. The manager and those who work with him have uncovered a disturbing fact that a component piece used in the assembly of the final project is not strong enough to meet the firm's stringent safety and quality standards.

The manager knows that if the project is undertaken there is a 60-40 chance of the component performing well. The manager writes the report and recommends that his department be given the work and that additional time and money be added to the budget to continue component development and vendor-research to ensure the safety and quality of the component.

The senior management of the firm reads the report and returns it to the manager with the requirement that he strike the section about delays and increases and instruct him to just factor the assembly of the component into the project. Senior management knows of the defect and believe that the client will not accept delays and costs increases. They want the project and the revenue it would bring to the firm. The manager is afraid of losing his job and is concerned about the jobs of those who work with him. He is worried that if he stands on his convictions he will be fired and the firm will go ahead with the project anyway. The manager rewrites the report and removes the reference to the component's safety and quality.

The employees who work with the manager read the report and quietly discuss the change in attitude and conviction of the manager. They question him. The manager justifies his action by stating his belief that the firm would have built the project without him and probably would have fired some of them as well. Therefore, it was a good decision.

This Beatitude implies that if we are truly seeking that which is good, right(eous), holy and equitable, when we find it—never let it go. We are called to commit our lives to Christ, even unto death. Can we not, at least, be willing to forfeit our jobs for Him?

Much of the world has forced Christianity to go underground. This Beatitude implies that if the underground Christian is discovered, he should defend his faith and continue that which he believes to be right. To do otherwise is to deny Christ. We should be willing to walk into the lion's den as Daniel did in the Old Testament. These are hard words to live up to. Many Christians have denied their faith to protect themselves, their spouses, children and friends. Many have justified their actions by saying that the underground church will grow stronger in spite of them.

In contrast, many "would-be" martyrs of the past looked at this line of reasoning and decided that it must be good to be persecuted—for any reason. Thus they set out to disturb the world. Baker described it best:

> *But our Lord did not say, "Blessed are the cantankerous." Others incur persecution, not by virtues which transcend conventional standards but by wickedness which falls below them. There were three crosses on Calgary, but only one man hung there for righteousness' sake. "We receive the due reward of our deeds," confessed one of the others to his companion, "but this man hath done nothing amiss" (1963, p. 82).*

The benefit of this Beatitude is incredible. Other Beatitudes asked the manager to know God, see God, become a son of God. Now, this Beatitude offers the entire Kingdom of Heaven. The increase in the "ante" represented by this Beatitude is a strong indicator of the importance God places on commitment to integrity. This is the essence of the phrase: "If you talk the talk, walk the walk."

Living a managerial life according to the Beatitudes can be exacting. Consider the following passage from Matthew 10:32-39 which Jesus said later in this same sermon:

"Whoever acknowledges me before men, I will also acknowledge him before my Father in heaven. But whoever disowns me before men, I will disown him before my Father in heaven.

"Do not suppose that I have come to bring peace to the earth. I did not come to bring peace, but a sword. For I have come to turn

> *"'a man against his father,*
> *a daughter against her mother,*
> *a daughter-in-law against her mother-in-law—*
>> *a man's enemies will be the members of his own household.'*

"Anyone who loves his father or mother more than me is not worthy of me; anyone who loves his son or daughter more than me is not worthy of me; and anyone who does not take his cross and follow me is not worthy of me. Whoever finds his life will lose it, and whoever loses his life for my sake will find it."

The words are clear. Do not place more value on anything, or anyone, than you place on God. This is acted out in the behavior of the manager when he does not place his own security, or that of his family or employees, before what he knows to be right(eous), good or equitable.

There is one balancing thought which the manager must understand. There is a difference between desires and values. In the component scenario above, the manager believed that he wanted to add five more staff to his group in order to complete the project, and he told his employees that he would get the additional people or resign. He must submit to his superiors unless the submission causes him to violate scriptural principles. The intelligent manager seeking righteousness should also possess wisdom and discernment to know the difference between wants and values. The foolish manager replaces integrity with pride and when challenged on pride preserves it to his own demise. Many managers have difficulty separating integrity issues from stubbornness.

Conclusion

Why should the manager who practices what is right expect persecution? Look at the paradox of what Christ is teaching. The manager should:

- be humble in a prideful world;
- have great concern and depth of feeling in a world where "me first" and stepping on fingers on the way up the ladder of success is the norm;

105

- demonstrate controlled discipline in a world where aggressiveness and outrage is common;
- seek what is right in a world where most seek what is self-gratifying, even at the expense of the firm and employees;
- be merciful in a world of revenge;
- have integrity above all, when situational ethics and the lack of absolutes are accepted as the only absolute;
- seek unity and diffuse conflict in a torn world filled with strife.

The manager acting in this paradigm would stick out like a sore thumb. The manager who follows the Beatitudes may become a threat to peers and superiors who do not understand the Beatitudes. The threat comes as he grows in success and popularity with those who serve with him. This may even increase the persecution. The unsuccessful many times seek ways of bringing down the successful in order to lift themselves up. It is pitiful that for so many the only way up is seen as a relative position to all others. If the unsuccessful cannot climb up the mountain, then they will bring the mountain down.

Those antagonistic to God and Christians persecute them as a means of genocide. We saw the attempts to accomplish this throughout the communist world. God provided blessings to the remnant which persevered and kept the faith.

Christ's call to live a life exemplifying His principles became a clarion call to the manager when He spoke those words on the mountainside. The call is as strong today as then. The principles are absolutes, unmovable, still offering the prizes of Heaven. Managers seek gold, oil, power, prestige, money and fame when the greater gifts are available if we would but change our lives and our behavior and follow the One who died for us.

Management writers of today cry out for role models, mentors, and leaders with a human touch. Christ gave the guidelines for success in this afternoon speech from the side of a mountain to a group of people gathered to hear the man from Galilee whom so many others talked about. Managers are unable to live out the Beatitudes alone. Jesus never told us we could survive this world and the next alone. We need the strength, power and grace that only He gives. No manager is complete without the strategic alliance of the Holy Spirit working in his life.

Consider your own managerial life. Ask yourself where you have not quite measured up to the benchmark of success. Ask God for help today in the continual improvement process.

Author's postscript

I began this essay from an interest in what the Beatitudes might say about management. I was not prepared for the depth of what I found. The Beatitudes are the opening lines to what is described as the "Sermon on the Mount." This sermon is considered to be the handbook for ethical living where righteous relationships are built and maintained between men and between God and man. I encourage you to read the remainder of The Sermon on the Mount and look for information on becoming an excellent manager.

Also, I encourage you to read this essay again from the perspective of what you would like to be known as when your time in management is over. Sort of a managerial epithet: *"Here was ..."* The blessings that the Beatitudes offer can be taken with you, gold and titles cannot.

Sources Consulted

Augsburger, Myron S. The Communicator's Commentary—Matthew. Lloyd J. Oglivie, General Editor. Waco, TX: Word Publishers, 1982.

Baker, Eric. The Neglected Factor—The Ethical Element in the Gospel. New York, NY: Abingdon Press, 1963.

Barclay, William. The Gospel of Matthew—Vol. I. Philadelphia, PA: The Westminster Press, 1958.

Batdorf, Irvin W. Interpreting the Psalms. Philadelphia, PA: The Westminster Press, 1966.

Bauman, Dan. Which Way to Happiness? Ventura, CA: Regal Books, 1981.

Blanchard, Ken, and Sheldon Bowles. Raving Fans. New York, NY: Morrow, 1993.

Boice, James Montgomery. The Sermon on the Mount. Grand Rapids, MI: Zondervan, 1972.

Buttrick, George Arthur, Commentary Editor. The Interpreter's Bible—Volume VII. New York, NY: Abingdon Press, 1951.

Kissinger, Warren. The Sermon on the Mount: A History of Interpretation and Bibliography. Metuchen, NJ: The Scarecrow Press, Inc, 1975.

Kodjak, Andrej. A Structural Analysis of the Sermon on the Mount. New York, NY: Mounton de Gruyter, 1986.

McArthur, Harvey K. Understanding the Sermon on the Mount. New York, NY: Harper & Brothers, 1960.

Robertson, Pat. The Secret Kingdom. Waco, TX: Word Books, 1992.

Schuller, Robert. The Be(Happy) Attitudes. Waco, TX: Word Books, 1985.

Strecker, George. The Sermon on the Mount—An Exegetical Commentary. Translated by O. C. Dean, Jr. Nashville,TN: Abingdon Press, 1988.

Strong, James. Abingdon's Strong's Exhaustive Concordance of the Bible. Nashville,TN: Abingdon Press, 1890.

Windisch, Hans. The Meaning of the Sermon on the Mount—A Contribution to the Historical Understanding of the Gospels and to the Problem of Their True Exegesis. Translated by S. MacLean Gilmour. Philadelphia, PA: The Westminster Press, 1951.

Winston, Bruce. The Master Management Builder and His Structure: A Story of Walls, Arches and Learning, an unpublished manuscript, 1993.

APPENDIX B: STUDIES IN BUSINESS

Why Work?[1]

1. Relationship with God

A. God orders man to work. God gave man dominion over the earth and entrusted the stewardship of his creation to man.

Supporting verses:

Gen. 1:28; Psalm 8:3-7 Dominion

Gen. 2:5,15 Stewardship

Gen. 3:17-19 Result of Adam's sin

Ex. 20:9 God's order

B. Work brings praise to God as we offer our bodies as living sacrifices.

Supporting verses:

Rom. 12:1-2 I appeal to you therefore, brethren, by the mercies of God, to pre-

---

sent your bodies as a living sacrifice, holy and acceptable to God.... (RSV)

Col. 3:23-24 Whatever your task, work heartily, as serving the Lord and not men, knowing that from the Lord you will receive the inheritance as your reward; you are serving the Lord Christ. (RSV)

2. Consideration of self and family

A. An individual must work in order to provide for his own and his family's living needs.

Supporting verses:

1 Tim. 5:8 Provide for your family.

Prov. 6:6-11; 10:4; 14:23 Diligence yields riches; laziness yields poverty.

B. Self-actualization: Man is composed of body, soul and spirit. As he exercises each part, he experiences the joy of doing what God made him to do.

Supporting verses:

Psalm 128:2 When you shall eat the fruit of your hands, you will be happy and it will be well with you. (NIV)

Eccl. 5:12 The sleep of the working man is pleasant, whether he eats little or much. (NIV)

3. Consideration of others

A. Diligent work helps one to create a surplus that he can share with others.

Supporting verse:

Eph. 4:28 Let him who steals steal no longer; but rather let him labor, performing with his own hands what is good, in order that he may have something to share with him who has need. (NIV)

B. Diligent work sets a positive example for others.

Supporting verses:

1 Thess. 2:9 Paul worked so that he wouldn't be a burden to those to whom he was preaching. His actions "preached" as loudly as his words.

2 Thess. 3:6-13 Paul described his work as a model for others.

Principles of Personal Work Ethics[2]

1. Love God: Love Him with all of your being. Honor, obey and glorify Him in everything.

Supporting verses:

> *Deut. 6:5* Love the Lord your God with all your heart and with all your soul and all your strength. (NIV)

> *Matt. 22:37* Jesus replied: "Love the Lord your God with all your heart, with all your soul, with all your mind." (NIV)

> *Mark 12:30; Luke 10:27* "And you shall love the Lord your God with all your heart, and with all your soul, and with all your mind, and with all your strength." (RSV)

Application:

> *Psalm 18:1-3* I love you, O Lord, my strength. The Lord is my rock, my fortress and my deliverer; my God is my rock, in whom I take refuge. He is my shield and the horn of my salvation, my stronghold. I call to the Lord, who is worthy of praise and I am saved from my enemies. (NIV)

---

[2] *Copyright 1989 by John E. Mulford. All rights reserved. Used with permission of the author.*

Psalm 34:1-3 I will bless the Lord at all times; His praise shall continually be in my mouth. My soul shall make her boast in the Lord: the humble shall hear thereof, and be glad. O magnify the Lord with me, and let us exalt his name together. (KJV)

Psalm 116:1 I love the Lord, because he has heard my voice and my supplications. (RSV)

2. Attitudes: Rejoice in the Lord always. Produce the fruits of the Spirit at all times, in all circumstances.

Supporting verses:

Gal. 5:22-23 But the fruit of the Spirit is love, joy, peace, patience, kindness, goodness, faithfulness, gentleness, self-control. (NIV)

Phil. 4:4,5,8 Rejoice in the Lord always. I will say it again: Rejoice! Let your gentleness be evident to all. The Lord is near... Finally, brothers, whatever is true, whatever is noble, whatever is right, whatever is pure, whatever is lovely, whatever is admirable— if anything is excellent or praiseworthy— think about such things. (NIV)

Psalm 68:3 But let the righteous be joyful; let them exult before God; let them be jubilant with joy! (RSV)

Isa. 51:11 Therefore the redeemed of the Lord shall return, and come with singing unto Zion; and everlasting joy shall be upon their head: they shall obtain gladness and joy; and sorrow and mourning shall flee away. (KJV)

Application:

Neh. 2:1-2,19-20; 4:14; 6:1-14 Nehemiah remained optimistic in the face of ridicule, harassment and threats of slander and physical violence.

3. Excellence: Strive for excellence in all your activities.

Supporting verses:

Prov. 22:29 Do you see a man skilled in his work? He will serve before kings; he will not serve before obscure men. (NIV)

Col. 3:17 And whatever you do, whether in word or deed, do it all in the name of the Lord Jesus, giving thanks to God the Father through him. (NIV)

Col 3:23 Whatever you do, work at it with all your heart, as working for the Lord, not for men. (NIV)

Application:

Gen. 41:46; Dan. 1:19-20 Joseph and Daniel rose to high positions under foreign kings because of their excellence.

4. Integrity: Tell the truth, keep your promises, and be loyal to your organization and colleagues.

Supporting verses:

Psalm 15:2,5 He whose walk is blameless and who does what is righteous, who speaks the truth from his heart...He who does these things will never be shaken.

Prov. 10:9 He who walks in integrity walks securely, but he who perverts his ways will be found out.

Prov. 11:3 The integrity of the upright guides them, but the crookedness of the treacherous destroys them. (RSV)

Prov. 20:7 A righteous man who walks in his integrity—blessed are his sons after him!

Isa. 33:15-16 He who walks righteously and speaks uprightly, who despises the gain of oppression, who shakes his hands, lest they hold a bribe, who stops his ears from hearing of bloodshed and shuts his eyes from looking upon evil, he will dwell on the heights; his place of defense will be the fortresses of rocks; his bread will be given him, his water will be sure. (RSV)

Titus 2:7-8 In everything set them an example by doing what is good. In your teaching show integrity, seriousness and soundness of speech that cannot be condemned, so that those who oppose you may be ashamed because they have nothing bad to say about us. (NIV)

Application:

Gen. 6:9 Noah was a man of integrity.

Gen. 39 Joseph showed his integrity in serving Potiphar and resisting Potiphar's wife.

4a. Truth

Supporting verses:

Prov. 12:22 The Lord detests lying lips, but he delights in men who are truthful. (NIV)

> *Eph. 4:25* Therefore each of you must put off falsehood and speak truthfully to his neighbor, for we are all members of one body. (NIV)

> *Zech. 8:16* These are the things that you shall do: speak the truth to one another, render in your gates judgements that are true and make for peace. (RSV)

> *Eph. 4:15* Rather, speaking the truth in love, we are to grow up in every way into him who is the head, into Christ.

Application:

> *Jer. 21* Jeremiah told the king exactly what God told him, even though it was terrible news that would surely not be will received. The prophets and apostles repeatedly told the truth without regard for the consequences.

4b. Promises

Supporting verses:

> *Matt. 5:37* Simply let your yes be yes, and your no be no. (NIV)

> *Num. 30:2* When a man makes a vow to the Lord or takes an oath to obligate himself by

a pledge, he must not break his word but must do everything he said. (NIV)

Application:

Josh. 2; 6:25   Joshua's spies kept their promise to spare Rahab's family.

Josh. 9   Joshua unwittingly promised the Gibeonites no harm, thinking they were foreigners. He broke God's command to kill everyone in the land in order to keep his promise to the Gibeonites.

Judg. 11:29-40   Jephthah foolishly promised to sacrifice the first thing to come out of his house if God would give him victory. He had to sacrifice his daughter to keep that promise.

4c. Loyalty

Supporting verses:

Psalm 101:6   My eyes will be on the faithful in the land, that they may dwell with me; he whose walk is blameless will minister to me. (NIV)

Prov. 28:20   A faithful man will abound with blessings, but he who hastens to be rich will not go unpunished. (RSV)

Matt. 25:23 His master said to him, "Well done, good and faithful servant; you have been faithful over a little, I will set you over much; enter in the joy of your master." (RSV)

Luke 16:10 "He who is faithful in a very little is faithful also in much; and he who is dishonest in a very little is dishonest also in much." (RSV)

Application:

1 Sam. 19:1-2; 20:4, 30-32 Jonathan and David were loyal to each other.

5. Responsibility

Supporting verses:

Gen. 2:15 The Lord God took the man and put him in the Garden of Eden to work it and take care of it. (NIV)

Luke 12:48 From everyone who has been given much, much will be demanded; and from the one who has been entrusted with much, much more will be asked. (NIV)

Application:

Gen. 39, 41 Joseph accepted the responsibility of managing Potiphar's house and later, all of Egypt. He proved an excellent steward of both.

Neh. 1-6 Nehemiah took on the responsibility of rebuilding Jerusalem's walls, and accomplished the task with few resources in the face of many obstacles.

6. Authority

Supporting verses:

Gen. 1:26 Then God said, "Let us make man in our image, in our likeness, and let them rule over the fish of the sea and the birds of the air, over the livestock, over all the earth, and over all the creatures that move along the ground." (NIV)

Rom. 13:1 Everyone must submit himself to the governing authorities, for there is no authority except that which God has established. The authorities that exist have been established by God.

Heb. 13:17 Obey your leaders and submit to them; for they are keeping watch over your souls, as men who will have to give account. Let them do this joyfully, and not sadly, for that would be of no advantage to you. (RSV)

1 Pet. 2:13-15 Be subject for the Lord's sake to every human institution, whether it be to the emperor as supreme, or to governors as sent by him to punish those who do wrong and to praise those who do right. For it is God's will that by doing right you should put to silence the ignorance of foolish men. (RSV)

Application:

Neh. 1-6 Nehemiah exercised the authority he was given as governor to its fullest.

Luke 7 The centurion understood the concept of authority. Paul submitted to Roman authority.

7. Service Leadership

Supporting verses:

Matt. 20:25-28 Jesus called them together and said, "Whoever wants to become great among you must be your servant, and whoever wants to be first must be your slave—just as the Son of Man did not come to be served, but to serve, and to give his life as a ransom for many." (NIV)

Luke 14:8-11 "When you are invited by anyone to a marriage feast, do not sit down in a place of honor, lest a more eminent man than you be invited; and he who invited you both will come and say to you, 'Give your place to this man,' and then you will begin with shame to take the lowest place. But... go and sit in the lowest place, so that when your host comes he may say to you 'Friend, go up higher'; then you will be honored in the presence of all who sit at table with you. For every one who exalts himself will be humbled, and he who humbles himself will be exalted." (RSV)

John 13:14-15 If I then, your Lord and Teacher, have washed your feet, you also ought to wash one another's feet. For I have given you an example.... (RSV)

Phil. 2:3-4 Do nothing from selfishness or conceit, but in humility count others better than yourselves. Let each of you look...to the interests of others. (RSV)

Application:

Neh. 5:14-19 Nehemiah worked next to the laborers rebuilding the wall. He also shared his table and did not extract the governor's food allowance from the people.

1 Kings 12 Rehoboam rejected the people's plea to be a servant leader. He increased taxes and penalties. As a result, Jeroboam banished him to Judah and the kingdom was divided.

8. Love your neighbor

Supporting verses:

> *Lev. 19:18* Do not seek revenge or bear a grudge against one of your people, but love your neighbor as yourself.

> *Matt. 22:39* Love your neighbor as yourself. (NIV)

> *Luke 6:31* And as you wish that men would do to you, do so to them. (RSV)

> *Luke 6:35* Love your enemies, and do good ...expecting nothing in return; and your rewards will be great. (RSV)

> *John 13:34* A new commandment I give you; "Love one another. As I have loved you, so you must love one another." (NIV)

> *Rom. 13:9* The commandments...are summed up in this sentence, "You shall love your neighbor as yourself." (RSV)

> *Gal. 5:14* For the whole law is fulfilled in one word, "You shall love your neighbor as yourself." (RSV)

> *1 John 4:7* Beloved, let us love one another; for love is of God, and he who loves is born of God and knows God. (RSV)

Application:

> *Neh. 1:1-4* Nehemiah loved the Jews in Jerusalem. He wept when he heard their plight, and boldly asked King Artaxerxes if he could go to their aid.

> *Luke 10:25-37* The good Samaritan loved his neighbor enough to give his time and money to a stranger in need.

9. Reconciliation

Supporting verses:

> *Matt. 5:23-24* Therefore, if you are offering your gift at the altar and there remember that your brother has something against you, leave your gift there...go and be reconciled to your brother; then come and offer your gift. (NIV)

> *Eph. 4:26* In your anger do not sin. Do not let the sun go down while you are still angry. (NIV)

Application:

> *1 Sam. 1-22* David sought reconciliation with Saul even while Saul was trying to kill him.

10. Forgiveness

Supporting verses:

> *Matt. 6:14* For if you forgive men when they sin against you, your heavenly Father will also forgive you. (NIV)

> *Matt. 18:21-22* Then Peter came to Jesus and asked, "Lord, how many times shall I forgive my brother when he sins against me? Up to seven times? Jesus answered, "I tell you, not seven times, but seventy times seven." (NIV)

> *Mark 11:25* And whenever you stand praying, forgive, if you have anything against anyone; so that your father also who is in heaven may forgive you your trespasses. (RSV)

Application:

> *Acts 7:60* Stephen forgave those who stoned him to death.

Notes